MW00580801

What Some People Are Saying About
NUMISMATIC FORGERY. . .

"He tells me [as a collector] that he has set out to frighten me. He has succeeded in scaring me to death. This book is good, good, good!"

> — *old coot who hangs around in the lobby of the hotel across from the bus station.*

"Honest to God, I wish this book didn't exist — but since it does, I'm afraid I must have a copy. I won't be able to get by without one now. Sure to become a classic reference."

> — *geezer who plays checkers with the old coot who hangs around in the lobby of the hotel across from the bus station.*

"Engrossing, brilliantly written! We in the numismatic field have been needing a wake-up call addressing our vulnerability to forgery for some time. Larson has delivered more than a wake-up call — he has detonated an atomic bomb."

> — *kid who delivers newspapers to the hotel across from the bus station, and occasionally kibitzes checker games.*

"So about how long have you known this 'Larson' guy, and where exactly did you say he lives?"

> — *name not given, field agent for Federal Bureau of Investigation, U.S. Treasury Department.*

NUMISMATIC FORGERY

by: Charles M. Larson

- An illustrated, annotated guide to the practical principles,
methods, and techniques employed in the
private manufacture of rare coins -

NUMISMATIC FORGERY

by: Charles M. Larson

© 2004 Charles M. Larson

All rights reserved, including duplication of any kind or storage in electronic or visual retrieval systems. Written permission is required for reproduction, in whole or part, of this book.

ISBN 0-9742371-2-4
(softbound)

PUBLISHED BY
Zyrus Press
PO Box 17810
Irvine, CA 92623
1-888-622-7823

CONTENTS

Foreword . . . . *i*
Preface . . . . *v*
Introduction . . . . *xi*

Chapter One
Forgery, forgery, everywhere 1

Chapter Two
Tools, Equipment, & Other Resources 9

Chapter Three
Methods of Forgery: Alteration 25

Chapter Four
Methods of Forgery: Casting 39

Chapter Five
Methods of Forgery: Creating Dies, Part I 55

Chapter Six
Methods of Forgery: Creating Dies, Part II 81

Chapter Seven
Collars and Edge Marking 101

Chapter Eight
Planchets 119

Chapter Nine
Minting Machinery and Processes 135

Chapter Ten
Wear, Aging, and Patina 155

Chapter Eleven
Detection and Protection 163

Appendix 175
Glossary 179

FOREWORD

This book is dangerous. Why? It's a "cook book" on how to create counterfeits and alterations! If this book doesn't scare the bejabbers out of you as a numismatist, you must not have a pulse.

These were my thoughts as I first began to consume these pages, before I learned a valuable lesson about the importance of knowing and understanding the techniques Charles Larson explains in this wonderful book.

Recently the numismatic press has been focusing on whether the spectacular so-called "transitional error" of a 1959-D United States cent with a (1909-1958) wheatback reverse is a genuine, mint-produced article or counterfeit.

I first examined this coin over three years earlier, and in my heart I was sure that it was a counterfeit. Nothing about it seemed right, and it reminded me of what my mother always warned me about: "When something seems too good to be true, it usually is." The problem was that I didn't know how to explain to myself (or anyone else) any satisfactory way in which it could possibly have been created. I remember thinking the cent must have been struck from dies created by a spark erosion process, but in my experience such dies invariably show random "spikes" that occur from the EDM process — and there was no trace of such die flaws anywhere on this coin. Perhaps a very low current could have been applied to help reduce pitting?

Then a story broke in Salt Lake's *Deseret News*, September 5, 2002, about a letter sent by the convicted forger and murderer Mark Hofmann to his daughter. He was gloating about the upcoming sale of the unique 1959-D cent with the wheatback reverse being offered by the Goldberg Numismatic Auctions of Beverly Hills, California. They had it catalogued at (and I quote) "estimated value $25,000.00 up." It was he, he boldly claimed in the letter, who had made the coin — using a process known only to himself.

I was wrong about the spark erosion. Charles Larson introduced me through this book to an insidious process I am now convinced has to be the one that was used to make this counterfeit. He explains that it was struck from die "shells" created by electroplating, and the "light bulb" went on for me in my mind's eye as he systematically put together the pieces of the puzzle. It turns out that Larson extensively interviewed Hofmann many years earlier when he served as Hofmann's night shift prison guard at the Utah State Penitentiary. Not only did Larson learn about this die making process straight from the forger's mouth, he later acquired Hofmann's electroplating equipment from one of Hofmann's victims, who had received it as partial reparations from the Utah Court. A nearly empty bottle of nickel electrolytic plating solution was included in the box of chemicals that came with the equipment.

What did Hofmann use the nickel electrolytic plating solution for, you ask? Well, read Chapter Five. You will then understand how this coin was made.

You know, I was a little embarrassed that I hadn't figured it out earlier on my own, but that's like hindsight being 20/20. As the immediate Past President of the American Numismatic Association (ANA), as well as an experienced instructor on Counterfeit and Alteration Detection at the ANA School of Numismatics (Summer Seminar) for the past several years, I had pretty good reason to feel that I was familiar with just about everything out there capable of fooling many dealers or collectors. But Charles Larson, an astute researcher, experimenter, and writer, taught me a lesson with this book. And when I admit that a seasoned veteran like me can benefit from this book, I'm saying that any and all numismatists can. I plan to make it a standard part of the curriculum for my class on Counterfeiting and Alteration Detection at Colorado College, next to the ANA headquarters.

So don't let the perceived "cook book" style of this book scare you away. It has an unusual and fantastic point of view, in that Charles talks and writes like he's taking you step by step through each process and procedure as if you were in a class called "how to make counterfeits." Everyone can learn and benefit from this method by carefully studying this work. I only wish I could have read it years ago and saved myself the embarrassment of making a few wrong calls on counterfeits and alterations.

There really hasn't been a new book about counterfeits for years, and nothing like this, ever. It's high time we all realize the potential of being fooled and sharpen our forgery detection skills. This work is a giant first step in that direction and on the path of better understanding the complex and fascinating world of numismatics.

H. Robert Campbell
Past President, American Numismatic Association (1999-2001)

PREFACE

On the subject of this book...

For all of the high principles and noble sentiments that mankind has labored for millennia to aspire toward, the human heart (as someone, somewhere once said) is basically a larcenous bitch.

Now this is not to give weight to the cynic's claim that most people are dishonest. I don't believe that at all; in fact, I rather think just the opposite is true. But that doesn't mean that the larceny isn't there. The truth is that honest people are often fascinated by dishonest acts — especially when they are cleverly done.

We witness this simple fact of life countless times each day. Visit any large bookstore and listen to the *Ching!* of the cash register as crime stories, murder mysteries, and detective novels are sold by the truckload. Television sleuths match wits with brilliant criminals every night on prime time, while old movies like *The Thomas Crown Affair* or *Dirty Rotten Scoundrels* (one of my personal favorites) have long since turned the depiction of clever criminals getting away with crime into a formula for sure-fire box office success. We have made people like D. B. Cooper and Oliver North into national folk heroes — and the list goes on and on. People admire cleverness, and cleverness seems to be one of the most basic prerequisites in our cultural quest for entertaining illegality.

Somewhere in the middle of all this I discovered — probably without thinking much about it at the time — that I was no different from everyone else. Having a fondness for history, I had always been interested in numismatics. But the more I learned about how coins were made, the more I couldn't help but speculate about how they could be *illegally* made. Speculation turned to study, study soon developed into research, and research eventually blossomed into experimentation. I never crossed the line of *intent*, of course — never seriously considered actually *creating* numismatic forgeries — but I grew more and more intrigued by the ingenuity of the processes involved as I discovered them. Names like Carl Wilhelm Becker and Christodoulos became familiar to me, and I studied examples of their work, along with types of the original coins they copied from. I learned to adapt concepts from my own art background and workshop experience, and devised methods to duplicate the effects of both historic and modern minting practices. The whole area of numismatic forgery became a preoccupation, a favorite hobby, almost a borderline obsession.

But even though I considered the subject most interesting, and I felt pretty sure that others would likewise find it interesting, none of this really had very much to do with what made me finally decide to write this book. The thing that made up my mind and got me started was that I attended a local gun show.

I don't often go to gun shows anymore. Several years ago it wasn't unusual to come across something of historic interest or a reasonably priced antique to restore or engrave, but anymore the survivalists and paramilitary cliques have taken over the shows to the point where they just aren't as enjoyable as they used to be. But there I was anyway, browsing casually about, when I found myself glancing at the titles on a large table covered with books. *How to Build Silencers*; *How to Make a Mortar*; *How to Convert This, That, or Some Other Firearm Into a Fully Automatic Assault Weapon*; *How to Concoct 35 Different Explosives From Common Household Items*; and so forth and so on. I'm not kidding. Really.

"It's against the law to do any of the things described in these books," I observed naively. "How is it that you can sell them?"

"These are just reference books," I was told matter-of-factly. "We make all of this available to collectors and other interested persons for scholarly and academic purposes only, which is perfectly legal. We don't expect anyone to use the information from our books to create something illegal. That would be wrong."

This was said with such a straight face that for half a moment I could almost believe that collectors and scholars could generate enough interest to warrant the marketing of three photocopied sheets of paper showing a template for the sheet metal receiver of a Sten gun for fifteen dollars. But if I failed to be impressed by the sincerity of the argument, I could not escape the logic of it. For therein lies an altogether American paradox: It is perfectly legal to produce, sell, own, and read a book that describes how to create something that is absolutely illegal to produce, sell, own, or use. God bless the First Amendment. *(Ching!)*

I have to believe, though, that the subject of numismatic forgery is one that actually should be of legitimate interest as well as concern to anyone who is interested in coins. The reason is really quite simple: The creating of successful forgeries of rare and valuable coins is a great deal easier than most people realize, and very little sophisticated equipment is required. I've mentioned how I decided to pass on the information I have learned, but I believe the why is probably much more important.

It is simply this: To be forewarned is to be forearmed. If you can discover a good reason why you should be more cautious, you may better determine how to use more caution. Therefore, this is not a book about *forgeries*, it is a book about *forgery.* If you consider yourself to be a serious collector, investor, or dealer and the contents of this book don't frighten you, you have ice water in your veins.

Come join me then, and I'll show you how numismatic forgery is done.

*-from my clandestine workshop,
deep in the bowels of the
Wasatch Mountains.*

Charles M. Larson

DISCLAIMER

This is a reference book. It contains material that is made available to collectors and other interested persons for scholarly and academic purposes only. This is legal. Naturally, I don't expect anyone to use the information from this book to create something illegal. That would be wrong.

Also, I wish to stress that *absolutely no actual forgeries or forgery materials were created during the production of this book.* The information presented herein is the result of many years of practical and perfectly legitimate art and shop experience, combined with a good deal of personal study, research, interview, and theoretical experimentation. It is my opinion that the principles, techniques, and methods described in this book could be employed by a person possessing larcenous intent to fabricate high quality forgeries of numismatic items. No express guarantee to this effect, however, is made or implied.

You are going to read about things here that have probably never been written down before, much less published and offered as information to the general public. I feel obliged to point out that some of the methods described in the pages which follow could be dangerous if undertaken carelessly. *All of them are illegal.* None of them should be attempted.

So don't. Ok?

— The Author

"If I can produce something so correctly, so perfect that the experts declare it to be genuine, then for all practical purposes it is genuine. There is no fraud involved when I sell it."

— *convicted master forger Mark Hofmann as related during a personal interview given to the author at Utah State Prison in 1987.*

INTRODUCTION

The Perfect Forgery?

The 1959-D Wheatback Cent. Photo courtesy Steve Benson

In the summer of 2002, the readers of *Coin World* were introduced to a bizarre and freakish oddity — the existence of a "mule" consisting of the obverse of a 1959-D cent and the wheatback reverse of a cent from 1958 (or earlier). Nothing like it had ever turned up before. According to one version of the story, the coin had supposedly first caught the eye of a California man while sorting through a large jar of cents in the year 1986. This event — which occurred some twenty-seven years after the coin would have been made, is the earliest provenance that can be attributed to it. How such a spectacular and valuable error could have been created, how it escaped the mint, and how it managed to remain hidden for so long are questions that would be puzzled over and warmly discussed, but they would remain unanswered.

The specimen showed no evidence of post-mint tampering typical of trick coins or other alterations — no front/back solder seam on the edge, no "cup and saucer" parting line inside the rim. Examination determined that the coin had been machine struck on a homogenous planchet of proper pre-1962 alloy using separate obverse and reverse dies of professional quality. From all appearances the coin was an actual, unmodified product of the Denver Mint.

Or was it?

Bob Campbell, the recent past-President of the American Numismatic Association and a renowned specialist on counterfeit and forgery detection didn't think so. "Something about the coin just didn't seem right," Bob would say later. "The fabric was there and everything pretty much looked correct, but it just felt wrong — not a physical kind of 'feel', but more of a gut-like feeling."

When he examined the actual coin he noticed distinct die polishing marks visible on the field of the obverse and reverse, a phenomenon not uncommon to early die strikes that normally disappears as a die is broken in by use. This indicated that the coin was a very early strike — and this, coupled with the absence of any other examples having turned up after more than four decades — suggested that it was perhaps even a unique strike. But he knew that modern mint production methods are so rapid and automated that it would have been impossible to "accidentally" strike a single such coin. There would have to have been others, and even if one solitary coin had managed to survive the inspection process there would certainly have been a discovery of others and a record of the incident of their striking.

But of course there was no such record. Oversight practices have improved dramatically since the days when five 1913 Liberty Head nickels had been privately struck after hours at the Philadelphia Mint. Bob described to me a conversation he had once had with numismatic author Kevin Flynn, who had interviewed Frank Gasparro (Chief Engraver of the U.S. Mint and designer of the Memorial reverse). Gasparro had been present at the Denver mint in the days prior to and during the set-up and first strikings when the series was introduced in 1959. "Frank told him that the idea of a transitional error — an accidental 'mule' — was foremost on everyone's mind at the time," Bob said, "and they went to extraordinary lengths to assure that no such thing happened. Every piece of equipment, every die was inspected and re-inspected, over and over. Everybody was accountable to someone else. No one could have had even the slightest opportunity to introduce a rogue reverse die from the previous year. Gasparro was very adamant about that."

The pot was stirred shortly after the *Coin World* article appeared when the Salt Lake City *Deseret News* ran a story that suggested an intriguing alternative. Master forger Mark Hofmann, serving a life sentence at the Utah State Prison (and a subscriber to *Coin World*), had written a letter to his daughter boasting rather off-handedly that it was none other than he, in fact, who had manufactured the 1959-D wheatback cent mentioned in the article. Was this possible, everyone wondered?

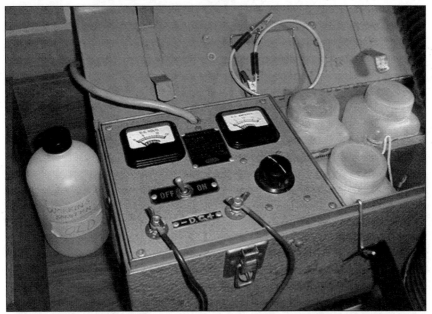

Was this electroplating machine, once owned by the notorious forger Mark Hofmann, used by him to create the enigmatic 1959-D Wheatback cent?

This was where I made a cameo appearance in the drama. Bob knew that I had been Hofmann's night sergeant years ago, back when I worked at the prison and he was first incarcerated. He also knew that I had mentioned having conducted many hours of casual interview with Mr. Hofmann during such times as I would let him out of his cell late at night so he could perform his tierman duties. (That would have been during 1986 -1987.) Bob was aware that we had talked extensively of history, of philosophy, and also of forgery. And he knew that Mark had described numismatic forgery techniques (some of which are included in this book) to me that had never been described to anyone else.

"Did Hofmann ever claim to have made this specific coin to you?" he asked me.

No, he had never specifically mentioned a Lincoln cent mule, but he did tell me that he used to make "error coins", and described a simple but ingenious method to me of creating dies by using an electroplating process.

"Do you think that the die making process he described is capable of producing a coin the quality of this one?"

Oh yes. Yes indeedy. I definitely do.

After that I remember being called by and speaking to reporters from *The Deseret News* and from *Coin World*, the auction house in Beverly Hills that was listing the coin for sale, and an agent from the Secret Service. To all of them I described the method just as Hofmann had described it to me, fifteen years earlier and before anyone had even imagined that such a process existed.

The eventual results were inconclusive, as the Secret Service had not been allowed to interview Hofmann, but had spoken only to his attorney.

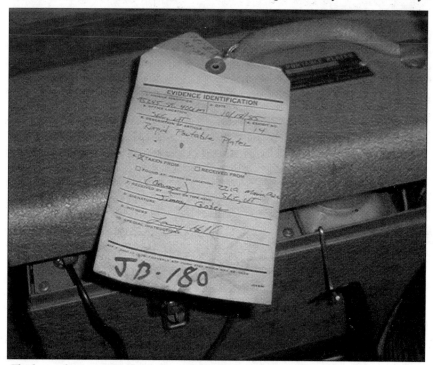

The law enforcement Evidence Tag is still attached to Mark Hofmann's electroplating machine, showing the date and location (Mark's garage) of its seizure.

The auction was delayed pending the Secret Service's investigation, and then conducted some months later after the Government stated that it could not prove that the coin was *not* a legitimate product of the U.S.

Mint. Interestingly, neither can the coin be *authenticated* by a professional grading service, since there is no other specimen to compare it to. I have been asked by a small number of people to attempt to duplicate the coin, a challenging task made even more interesting by the fact that I had some years earlier acquired the very electroplating machine that Hofmann had owned and used. As of this writing I feel comfortable stating that I am quite close to being able to announce my results.

But would the successful duplication of this coin, using the methods Hofmann described, prove once and for all that the 1959-D cent with a wheatback reverse is a forgery?

No, it would not. While it would demonstrate that the coin could have been created by a forger, it would still be simply a significant piece of evidence to add to a compelling argument the one way, only to be challenged by compelling argument the other way.

Proof, as any attorney can tell you, is sometimes a relative thing.

Chapter One

Forgery, forgery, everywhere . . .

Show a "bad coin" to the average person and ask, "Is this a counterfeit, or is this a forgery?" and you will probably get a puzzled look and an answer along the lines of, "So what's the difference?" But before we of the coin-wise world smile our superior smile and prepare to begin educating, let's back up a bit. That was actually a very valid question!

Whether the coin is a counterfeit or a forgery, it could look exactly the same. It could feel exactly the same. The exact same process could have been used to manufacture it, its alloy could be identical, its type the same — in fact, the *same coin* could be *either.* But not both. The answer, of course, lies not in what the coin is like, but in why it was made.

People who are involved with coins know this, but it is understandable why most other people would not. Numismatic definitions in this respect are usually much more precise than, say, the Court Reports section of the local newspaper. When we read about someone who is convicted for forging a prescription, we can be sure of two things: A) — the "prescription" was an unauthorized, illegally produced item, and B) — it was intended to serve the same purpose as a legitimate prescription. By numismatic standards, if the prescription were a coin it would be a *counterfeit* — not a forgery!

A *counterfeiter* might print up a stack of fake $20 bills and take off for Atlantic City or Lake Tahoe and try to spend them as $20 bills. Or he may create a sheet of his own postage stamps and use them to mail off his Christmas cards. The idea, of course, is that the counterfeit is intended to illegally serve the same purpose as the original item serves legitimately. To be regarded as successful, a counterfeit only needs to be accepted as authentic once — when passed by the counterfeiter to his victim.

A *forger*, on the other hand, would direct his talents toward creating a scarce $20 demand note from the Civil War, or an ultra-rare 1918 upside-down airmail stamp — and market them to a collector for hundreds, or even thousands of dollars. With the stakes so high, for a forgery to be considered successful it must be capable of not only passing but withstanding the scrutiny of experts. The longer a forgery goes undetected, the safer the forger is and the longer he can continue to operate.

What holds true for bills and stamps also holds true for coins, so let's return to our "bad coin" we started out with. Which is it? Well, regardless of the period in history the fake would date from if it were real, if it was manufactured recently (say, within the past 30 years) the odds are better than a thousand to one that it's a forgery. The reason is simple. Antique coins containing precious metals no longer circulate as money because their bullion value is much higher than their face value, and contemporary base metal coins have such a low face value (and no intrinsic value at all) that they are not worth counterfeiting. With very few exceptions — as in the case of noncirculating legal tender coins (more about that later) — the day of the counterfeit coin has passed. You needn't inspect your pocket change any more, *but* — the next time you purchase a collectable coin of *any* kind it wouldn't be a bad idea to examine it closely, because the day of the forged coin is bright and young and healthier than it has ever been.

Professional numismatists writing about forgery often make the point that while modern forgeries have become terribly good, to produce them requires new, expensive equipment, sophisticated techniques, and some sort of dark, secret knowledge available only from some kind of forger's version of Mount Olympus. Not so. As you will soon discover, successful numismatic forgery is actually much easier than you have been led to believe, and the information about how to do it has always been readily available if a person was simply willing to look for it. All of the methods and techniques described in this book were uncovered (or more or less stumbled upon) by — and let's be frank — an amateur. I have no hesitation in writing about them because I think practically anyone who wanted to could easily come up with the same things (or more!). Obviously, many have already. And as for the cost of equipment, you will soon see that just about anybody with even a moderate income could manage without too much difficulty to put together the basics necessary to get started.

But methods and equipment aside for a moment, the most critical element in numismatic forgery is the forger. Just how many of them are out there?

There is no way of ever knowing, of course. We know they are there because their forgeries keep turning up, but forgers don't form support groups or list their occupation in the Yellow Pages. About the best we can do is to try a little bit of reasonable interpolation to calculate just how many forgers — or at least *potential* forgers — there could be among us.

To start with, there are estimated to be about 280,000,000 people living in the United States, not counting the illegal aliens in California and Texas. We'll go with 280 million. Obviously not every one of them is a potential forger! Some are only children or babies, for instance. We'll need to trim the figure a bit. Different people could come up with different ways to start the disqualifying process, but I am going to suggest just four criteria:

1) Possession of adequate intelligence and creativity,

2) Artistically inclined, coupled with basic mechanical skills,

3) Interest in the subject, and

4) Larcenous intent.

The first hurdle is probably the touchiest one. People become very offended when you start classifying what they can or can't do on the basis of their intelligence (or lack of it), which is understandable. After all, no two people share exactly the same abilities, so at any given moment half the population has an IQ below average. I don't think a person needs to necessarily be a genius (IQ in the upper 1 or 2 percent range) to be a successful forger, but it is fair to expect that the demands of the task would fall to those in the "above average" category. That's half the population. Now let's eliminate the children and babies, tack on a qualifier for the creative streak, and if we are very conservative I think we can still comfortably say that 10% of the population possesses adequate intelligence as well as a tendency toward creativity. Now we're down to 28,000,000.

In the second category, we're not necessarily looking for professional artists. Some talent would certainly be helpful, but mainly we're looking for the ability to perceive artistically. To judge a composition, to compare and evaluate examples, to detect dissimilarities. Add to this the basic mechanical skills requirement, and I think we can put it again at 10%. Now we're down to 2,800,000.

That's two million, eight hundred thousand people in this country who are of above average intelligence, creative, artistically inclined, and possess basic mechanical skills. I don't think it's unreasonable at all to expect that another 10% of these would find history interesting — and if history, then certainly numismatics. And anyone interested in numismatics will also find numismatic forgery interesting. So now we're down to 280,000.

The last is the easiest. The latest figures I have (as of April, 1994) show that the national per capita rate of incarceration in the United States is 344 persons per 100,000 of the population. This equates to 3.44 per 1,000, or around 1/3 of a person per 100. Since obviously not all persons who *deserve* to be are incarcerated at any given time, I think it is quite safe to say that out of any group of a hundred people, there will be one, on the average, who possesses larcenous intent. One percent. This leaves us with 2,800 people in the United States who are prime, potential forgers of rare and valuable numismatic items.

Put another way, that's ten for every population of a million. Forty-five for the Los Angeles area *alone*. One for every community of a hundred thousand.

I live in an area of about a hundred thousand people, and for the past ten years or so we have had an average of four coin dealers serving our needs at any given time. I can't say whether this is typical of the rest of the country, but I suspect it probably isn't too far off the mark. If so, that makes one potential professional forger of coins for every four coin dealers in America.

Does this mean that there are that many? I doubt it. Remember, these are *potential* figures, and the actual number is probably only a fraction of that. But we don't know what fraction, and the fraction could easily grow, couldn't it? Starting to get nervous yet, collector? Investor? Well, read on, because there's more.

Modern numismatic forgery is not necessarily geared toward producing copies of the ultra-rare, the spectacular, or the extremely valuable. To the layman (who lacks larcenous intent) it might seem that the object of every forger would be to create an 1804 silver dollar or a 1913 Liberty head nickel, but the wise forger will want to attract as little attention as possible, either to himself or to his forgery. He[1] is aware that anything

---

[1] You may have noticed that I keep referring to forgers in the masculine sense. I'm not doing this intentionally to appear sexist, but merely to demonstrate our cultural perceptions when we think of crime in general.

excessively rare, spectacular, or valuable is almost certainly going to be submitted to an authentication service, probably even as a prior condition to purchase. The techniques covered in this book *could* be employed to create a 1964 Peace dollar or a muled 1946 Roosevelt dime with a 1945 reverse, but to what purpose? The ultimate undoing of most forgers who eventually become exposed is that they attracted too much attention. To remain safe, the forger's object should be to function anonymously, making a continuous, unnoticed income, rather than a one-time spectacular killing. Normally, he will achieve this by carefully considering the sort of forgeries he chooses to create, as well as the way he decides to market them.

This brings us to our first maxim — *the coins that forgers forge the most are those coins which buyers buy the most.* Small denomination U.S. gold coins of the 19th and early 20th century. Uncirculated or near-uncirculated U.S. type coins of common date, or well-circulated type coins of more scarce dates. Nicely struck but moderately worn and common ancients — especially Greek, Roman, and Biblical coins. Uncirculated commemoratives, and noncirculating legal tender gold coins. These are the sort of coins that are routinely bought and sold hundreds of times every day, and hardly merit a second thought from the typical purchaser of coins — a point not lost on the ambitious yet quiet forger. He knows if he keeps the asking price of his wares modest ($50 to $300 range) that he can expect an immediate sale, and that most coins of this sort are almost never submitted for authentication, since they are always easier for the buyer to turn around and resell if the cost of an authentication service does not have to be added to the coin.

The thought is probably crossing the minds of many readers right now that $50 to $300 for a forged coin isn't an awful lot of money, and that numismatic forgery is beginning to sound like something along the lines of an unprofitable hobby for the bored and reckless. I'll grant that this may not seem like much return for all of the effort, expense, and risk it takes to produce a forgery, so our second maxim is that *a forger will seldom produce just one of anything.* With the aid of a little imagination and an understanding of how most coins are bought and sold, a disturbing picture begins to emerge of just how a successful forger might operate.

To begin with, I see a casually dressed, ordinary looking person riding a bus from the airport to the downtown area of any large city. (It is said that even a bird will not foul its own nest, and only a fool would habitually market his forgeries in his own community.) He may have studied a local business directory and mapped out his route beforehand, or he may be playing it by ear; in any case, he has his routine down and is prepared to adapt to whatever conditions he encounters.

A typical pawnshop, common to every metropolitan area.

His objective, interestingly, is not a coin store or the place of an advertised coin dealer. He is headed instead to a part of town where pawnshops are plentiful — most of which display large signs announcing *We Buy Gold & Silver*. There are literally scores of such places in any sizable metropolitan area. Entering a likely appearing establishment, he asks the proprietor if they are buying any coins that day.

"Show me what you have," the pawnbroker will usually say.

Withdrawing a small paper envelope from his pocket, the forger opens it and gently shakes its contents out onto the countertop. He is careful to keep the envelope. The pawnbroker possibly winces slightly at the sight of collectable coins being carried around in such a way that they can rub against each other, and silently reaches the conclusion that his visitor knows very little about coins.

On the counter are perhaps three, and no more than five, small gold coins. They are superbly fashioned die-struck forgeries of U.S. quarter eagles and gold dollars, each showing light to moderate circulation wear, no two bearing the same date. Their weight and alloy are perfect — as they should be, for the planchets they were struck from were made by melting down a legitimate but heavily worn $20 gold piece. (The worn $20 gold piece, weighing about one Troy ounce, was purchased for less than fifty dollars over the spot price of the gold it contains. Each of the eight quarter eagle forgeries that can be made from it will bring the forger at least fifty dollars over spot, yielding him a total profit of $350. Each of the twenty gold dollar forgeries he can make from a similar coin will give him about a hundred dollars of profit apiece. He combines the two types of forgeries in a single lot for sale to alleviate suspicion.)

If asked where the coins came from, the forger may vaguely mumble something about an aunt or a grandmother. The pawnbroker doesn't really care. He examines the coins and sees that they are mostly common date varieties — though one bears a mint mark (look it up later!) — and concludes that the quarter eagles would have an A.B.P. (Average Buying Price) of $140 each, the gold dollars an A.B.P. of $175 each.

"Well, I can give you a hundred apiece for the lot," the pawnbroker might say. The forger agrees that this certainly sounds fair, accepts the three to five 100-dollar bills handed to him, lingers a moment or two while inconspicuously looking at used tools or musical instruments, and then leaves with the empty, forgotten envelope tucked back inside his pocket.

He may skip the next two or three places, but then the forger enters another pawnshop on the next block and repeats his performance. He will do this a dozen or so times that day, never expecting more than about $500 from any one place, sixty to ninety percent of which will be pure profit over his own costs. By that afternoon he is back at the airport boarding another plane. Twenty-four hours later he has just done the same thing all over again a thousand miles away.

As you can see, there are several effective techniques our forger uses that combine to contribute to the success of his method, but the key thing that makes it all believable is the *variety* of pieces he is able to offer simultaneously. When a buyer is presented with a group of different coins of different denominations with different dates, he is automatically lulled into the assumption that they are genuine. This makes it far easier (and safer) for a forger to attempt to sell a small number of moderately priced coins as a lot than a single, higher priced coin, even though the price of either might come out the same.

So our third maxim is that *just as forgers will seldom produce only one of anything, they will also seldom limit their production to any one thing.* In fact, if the forger we just looked at wanted to be particularly cautious, he could even prepare different forgeries for each buyer in any one city, so that no two "assortments" contained the same coins. For a dozen separate buyers at a time, this would mean having available an inventory of anywhere from forty to fifty different forged coin types. And this is not at all an impractical or unrealistic figure.

Provided he keeps track of what he has distributed and where, limits the number he produces of any single item, changes his wares occasionally, and never approaches the same buyer twice, there is no reason that a forger couldn't operate like this indefinitely.

Picture the number of numismatic forgeries that could be introduced into the coin marketplace in a single year by just one such professional forger. Now try to picture the effect of two dozen — or about half of what could be expected just for the city of Los Angeles. Now picture 2,800 of them.

And you begin to get the picture.

Chapter Two

Tools, Equipment, & Other Resources

Here we are, then, with 2,800 potential professional numismatic forgers all lined up at the starting gate and waiting for some sort of signal to take off. But to do just what, exactly? Their objective — to create effective forgeries of rare and valuable coins — may be perfectly clear to them, but the *how* and the *with what* are probably still a bit fuzzy to the rest of us. In this chapter we'll take a good look at the with what, before actually moving on to the how.

I have already mentioned that successful numismatic forgery requires very little sophisticated equipment. The truth is that if by "sophisticated" we mean exotic, expensive, or nearly impossible to obtain, then actually *none at all* is required! No three-dimensional pantographic reduction milling lathe, no turbine driven hydraulic stamping press, no electric melting furnace or strip rolling mill. For the majority of numismatic forgery, the difficult and expensive work which requires such equipment has *already been done for the forger by the government that produced the coins he is forging.*

This is not to say, however, that the forger's workshop will not be needing a few items of a "specialized" nature — or in other words, tools and equipment that are common enough, but which just may not be typically found in the average home workshop. Also, there are a number of devices that the forger will want to have that are so specialized that they may be considered unique, but all of these can easily be fabricated in his own shop, and so will be dealt with later on as we examine how they will be used.

Since coin making is essentially a process of metal fabrication, the forger's workshop is of necessity a metalworking shop. Most home workshops, on the other hand, are nowadays oriented toward either woodworking or mechanics. The forger, then, can expect to put away his scroll saw and wood chisels, his timing light and his socket set. He will find the following much more useful.

Lathe

It is hard for me to imagine any metalworking tool more important, more necessary, more *basic* than a lathe. I personally own three of them, and I am still discovering ways to use them that I hadn't thought of before. A lathe can be used for turning, drilling, boring, milling, grinding, scraping, shaping, reaming, polishing, punching, planing, tapping, threading, tapering, squaring, knurling, and God only knows what else. In fact, it has been said that a lathe is the only machine tool capable of reproducing itself, as every critical part of a lathe can be made on a lathe. (I haven't actually tried this yet, but I've made enough replacement parts here and there over the years to be able to agree.) Truly, the lathe is the "King of Tools", and the core of any metal shop.

And yet you hardly ever see one any more outside of a commercial machine shop. They used to be fairly common, say, fifty years ago, when the tastes of craftsmen ran more to building steam engines and model cannons than bookshelves and bird feeders. Sadly, a decent metal-working lathe suitable for the home workshop is no longer being manufactured in this country.

Older, used lathes are still around, though, and the forger really should have access to one. He could always contract out some of the machining work he will need to have done, of course, but there are certain jobs — like the finish turning of coin dies, for example, or the making of collars — that simply must be done in the privacy of his own shop. (As with any illegal activity, the more a forger does on his own, the less anyone else knows about what he does.)

So the forger needs a lathe. My three are fairly representative of what he can expect to find available.

1. Small Hobby Lathe

For many years a favorite of model railroaders and other hobbyists, these wonderful little lathes are capable of great precision, and have accessories that can convert the basic unit to a variety of machine shop tools, including a drill press, vertical milling machine, and more. Mine is an older model made by Unimat, which is no longer in business, but its updated successor is presently being produced and marketed by Sherline. Advertisements for the new machine can be found in most hobby magazines, and used units can often be found for sale through various modeling clubs.

The small hobby lathe is barely adequate for numismatic forgery.

Ideal for what they are designed for — miniature machining — the biggest drawback to them is that they are simply too small and underpowered for most typical machine shop work. The forger would be able to finish turn dies and make collars and other small items on one of these lathes, but he would be severely limited when it came to doing much else, and he would be completely unable to create many of the larger, specialized tools described in this book. I would have to rate the small hobby lathe as *barely adequate*.

2. Mid-sized Lathe

Usually referred to "bench" lathes because they were meant to be mounted on a workbench, these machines are slightly scaled-down versions of a full-sized lathe, with all of the features, functions, and capabilities of their larger counterparts. They are the perfect size for the home workshop, which is precisely the purpose they were made for by companies like South Bend, Sheldon, Atlas, and several others. If a person is fortunate enough to come across one of these (and the owner is foolish enough to part with it), they would be smart to grab it — quick.

My bench lathe was put out by Sears, and is basically an Atlas lathe sold under the Sears trade name. Sears stopped carrying these sometime in the early '70s, which is a real shame because it was the last lathe of its kind on the market. I was able to pick mine up very used from a fellow who'd gotten it as part of a trade for something or other. Since it didn't seem to work, he thought he was doing well to ask $50 for it! I cleaned it up, painted it, and had the motor rewired, and now you couldn't talk me out of it for twenty times as much. It is well made, extremely accurate, easy to use, marvelously versatile, and takes up very little shop space.

The mid-sized lathe is an excellent choice for numismatic forgery.

With a similar unit and the necessary attachments, a forger would be able to perform almost any machining work he would ever find necessary. For the purposes of numismatic forgery, I will rate the mid-sized bench lathe as *excellent*.

3. Full-sized Lathe

Also known as "tool room" lathes, these are industrial quality lathes with every feature of a bench lathe except that they are larger, have more power, and a greater work capacity. Since they are necessary for commercial and industrial work, full-sized lathes are still being manufactured, though with features such as infinitely variable speed control and computer guided cutting tools, they can be quite expensive. Often, though, a used older lathe can be located for a much more reasonable price, and it will give service every bit as good as the newer models.

My full-sized lathe was made in 1942 by South Bend under a War Department contract for the U.S. Navy, and I understand it was used on board a submarine during World War II. Its operation is smooth, sure, and flawless in every respect. Provided he has the space (it requires nearly an entire wall), this type of lathe is capable of doing everything the forger could possibly require. For the purposes of numismatic forgery, I rate the full-sized tool room lathe as *ideal.*

The full-sized lathe is ideally suited for numismatic forgery.

Whichever type of lathe the forger chooses or ends up with, if he has never operated one before he will need to learn how. Most high schools or community colleges offer evening classes that include Industrial Education (Machine Shop), and this could even be a possible source for leads in obtaining equipment. Also, any good used bookstore should be able to locate an old copy of *Machinist's Guide* or a similar work, which will be an excellent source of useful information that never goes out of date. My copy of *Audels Machinists and Tool Makers Handy Book* (sic), printed in 1941, is an incredibly comprehensive collection describing basic and advanced machine tool operations, metalworking techniques, and practical instruction that would likely cost hundreds of dollars to compile and present today. I think I might have paid about four dollars for it.

Drill Press

This is another very basic machine shop tool, and is much more convenient and accurate to use than a hand electric drill. They are also quite plentiful and reasonably priced, so many home workshops will already have one.

The forger will use it primarily in the manufacture of other forgery equipment, so he will probably want one with a 1/2 inch chuck, variable speed capability, and a good, sturdy vise to hold his work.

Typical drill press - an easy to obtain item. (The rotary compound table is an extravagance.)

High Speed Rotary Hand Tool

In other words, a Dremel (or similar) tool. I like the type that has a flexible shaft and variable speed control, with interchangeable collets for holding the bits and mandrels. These tools are so useful that I've included it more or less automatically, even though I don't have any specific task for it in mind that is related exclusively to forgery, except maybe for fine grinding the edges of punches. I don't recommend it for engraving, though — that is best done by hand. But for precision sharpening of tool bits, cutting screw slots, and trimming stock, this tool is pretty much indispensable.

Rock Tumbler

This is an inexpensive, sealed rubber drum that rotates at a slow speed for several hours (or days, or weeks) at a time, gently tumbling and smoothing and wearing down whatever has been placed inside of it. The forger will find it useful for polishing blank planchets just prior to striking them, and also for duplicating the effect of years of "circulation" on coins in a matter of days. These can be found at lapidary shops (where rocks and jewelry supplies are sold), and they are also carried by many gun stores, where they are used to polish cartridge cases.

An older type lapidary rock tumbler. The rubber drum seals to contain liquid or dry tumbling medium.

Kiln

Here is an example of a specialized tool that most people don't have — or if they do, they probably have a pottery kiln that loads from the top and uses heat sensitive cones to regulate the temperature. This won't do. The type of kiln a forger will find useful is also known as a "bake-out oven", and has a front-loading door and a temperature graduated pyrometer on the outside. The forger doesn't need a very large one, as he will use it primarily for pre-heating crucibles and burning out molds during the lost wax casting process. It is also an excellent means of heat treating metals to exact temperatures. This kind of kiln can be obtained, along with the next item, from jewelry manufacturing supply sources.

A front-loading kiln, or "bake out oven", designed for lost wax casting.

Centrifuge

A centrifugal casting machine may at first sound like a very exotic and sophisticated piece of equipment, but it is actually an extremely simple device. All a metal casting centrifuge consists of is a horizontal spinning bar mounted on a pivot post at its center. This post is set into a spring-wound base, which has a combination lock bar/release catch on it. At one end of the horizontal bar the empty mold is mounted, with the crucible for the molten metal directly in front of it. When the machine is wound up and released, the molten metal is thrown by centrifugal force into the cavity of the mold, where it remains under pressure as it cools and solidifies.

And that's all there is to one. Jewelers use them to make rings for your fingers and dentists use them to make crowns for your bridgework. They aren't particularly expensive, but considering how little there is to one of them I still think they're overpriced.

Centrifugal casting produces superior detail using the lost wax process, but the casting method by itself is incapable of creating forgeries that are undetectable. Still, the forger is able to use lost wax casting very effectively, but not in the way you would probably imagine! More about this later, though.

This centrifuge is somewhat larger than one would normally come across - it is a commercial model intended for jewelry manufacture. Much smaller models are also made in many styles, but all operate basically the same.

Vacuum Table

There isn't much to one of these, either — a rubber mat with a hole in the middle, laying on a base with a small vacuum pump under it. A glass or plastic dome to fit over the top. And that's all.

A vacuum table is used to evacuate all of the tiny air bubbles that become trapped while mixing up investment plaster or pourable rubber mold compounds. Unless they are removed, these bubbles can create voids in a mold that will mar the surface of the object being cast. Care in mixing and mold preparation will also prevent most of these bubbles, though, so a vacuum table isn't an absolute necessity.

This homemade vacuum table is just as effective as a commercial model.

Pantograph

This is yet another example of an utterly simple tool which, because it is used in jewelry manufacture, is priced higher than it has a right to be. Basically all there is to it is an arrangement of hinged levers set up on a small base. By moving a guide on the forward part of the levers along a pattern, a point mounted in the center of the levers will reproduce the same pattern on a smaller scale.

A pantograph isn't absolutely necessary for most numismatic forgery either, but it can be quite helpful for engraving small detail when making punches, such as for mint marks, or for doing layout work if the forger engraves his own dies by hand.

This pantograph is set up for tracing a pattern for a portrait punch. (To view the finished punch, see Chapter Five.)

Electroplating Unit

Quite a bit of successful numismatic forgery can be accomplished without any electroplating equipment at all, but a pretty fair amount can also be done with very little else.

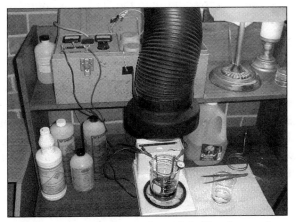

An electroplating unit set up to plate nickel. (Note the vent above the beaker for evacuating fumes.)

There is nothing mysterious or complicated about electroplating. A small jar or beaker, a couple of feet of wire, some clamps, a 12 volt dry cell battery, small strips of the metal being used to plate to serve as anodes, solutions of acidic plating baths, and some insulating varnish are all that is required. The entire process can be set up and take place on the top shelf of a closet behind a closed and locked door.

Different plating baths are used with different anodes. Those most useful to the forger will be silver, gold, copper, and nickel.

Oxygen/Acetylene Torch

Another one of those basic items that has a place in every metal fabricating shop. In manufacturing the specialized tools and equipment he will use for forgery, the forger will find it useful for cutting, welding, brazing, and soldering, as well as for heat treating (annealing, hardening, and tempering). It will also come in handy for melting metal for planchets and lost wax casting.

With so many tasks to perform, the forger will need to select a unit that has an assortment of torch tips — cutting, welding, and flood heating — as well as an adequate gas capacity. He needn't encumber himself with the larger industrial sized models that are around, but he should expect to get something a bit more substantial than the "propane bottle" sized torches that many hardware stores carry. The tiny hand held "needle" torches are practically worthless for serious heating, but they can still be useful for precision spot soldering — if they are handled with extreme care.

Since a nominal oxygen/acetylene torch unit can do whatever small amount of welding the forger may find necessary, I haven't bothered to list separately a small arc-welding unit, even though many people find arc welding to be easier than gas welding. The forger may choose whichever method he wishes for his welding, of course, but he will still need the torch for the other things mentioned.

Optivisor (TM)

Jewelers, modelers, numismatists, and many others can attest to the great usefulness and practicality of this wonderful vision aid. It consists if a pair of binocular magnifying lenses mounted in a visor, allowing its wearer to work with both hands free while comfortably viewing objects 2 or 3 times their normal size. A small swivel lens over one eye may be lowered to provide ten-power magnification for close inspection of small areas. I have used one for many years for engraving and miniature work, and I will state flat out that I would never attempt to do fine detail work of any sort without one. They can even be worn over normal glasses. The advantage that the use of one of these could give to the forger should be self-evident.

I couldn't get by without one of these.

Jeweler's Loupe

While the Optivisor Provides ample magnification to work by, close examination of numismatic items by collectors is normally done with a jeweler's loupe. At 16X magnification the tiny nicks and scratches invisible to the eye, the flow of the metal around the mint mark, and the symmetry of the reeded edge all pop out with vivid and distinguishing clarity. I have never failed to see a dealer prepare to purchase even a moderately priced coin without first studying it through a loupe.

Since collectors and dealers are familiar with how a genuine coin should look through a jeweler's loupe, the forger must be also. If his forgeries cannot pass a detailed visual examination, they will be exposed the first time he offers them.

Jeweler's loupes are available in various magnifications; a good standard is 16X.

Machinist's 6" Calipers

Accurate measurements are critical to accurate work. Since a forger's work will be compared against the standard of the coins it represents, the forger must first measure and record those standards from genuine coins and then adapt his forgeries to match them.

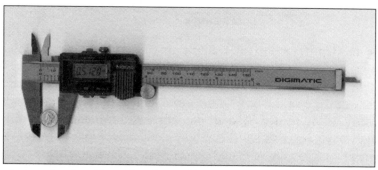

Again, an item I would consider indispensable.

This cannot be done with cheap or poorly made measuring devices. The plastic type of 6" calipers that are commonly found in hardware stores are only accurate to about a hundredth of an inch — which is woefully inadequate for good precision work. Well-made machinist's calipers typically measure to within five ten thousandths of an inch (or a thousandth of a millimeter). I like the digital type that will convert from inches to millimeters and back by pressing a small button.

Reloader's Scales

Also necessary to take accurate measurements, and for checking the weight of planchets, etc. Sporting goods stores and gun shops sell supplies for reloading ammunition to shooters and sportsmen, and offer a small, reasonably priced powder scale that is accurate to within a tenth of a grain — that's 0.0002285 oz!

10' Diameter Tape

No, this isn't a tape that is ten feet in diameter. It's a ten-foot long, thin, narrow measuring tape that is graduated in π increments of inches on its reverse side. By wrapping it around any round object, both the circumference (to the nearest 1/320") and the diameter (to the nearest 1/100") can be determined. Coins are generally too small to be conveniently or accurately measured this way, but the 10' diameter tape becomes very useful to the forger when making an index plate in order to create an accurate reeded edge for collars.

Work Bench

Needn't be large or elaborate — anything from a desktop to a kitchen table will certainly suffice. A comfortable work bench, though, should generally be about waist high, and sturdy enough to support the work that is done on it. A 6" bench grinder mounted on one end and a vise mounted on the other will finish it off, along with an assortment of hand files and other minor tools.

Facilities

Any honest person innocently assembling a home workshop could take all of the items listed above and arrange them in just about any space he has available: a garage, a basement, a spare room — or even a shed, if he wanted — and it wouldn't really matter. His only real concern would be to take precautions to prevent theft. But a forger, who possesses larcenous intent, must necessarily be concerned with privacy as well as security. Walls, covered windows, and locks will therefore be as much a feature of his work space as his tools and equipment.

Mark Hofmann, the notorious document forger, used to do most of his work in a small, windowless room in his basement, which he kept locked at all times. Even his wife was reportedly never allowed to enter his "study". It may not always be possible for the numismatic forger to prevent others from knowing that he has a workshop, but he must certainly find a way to keep what he does there a secret.

And those are the basics. As you can see, there is nothing particularly exotic, complicated, or inordinately expensive among them, nor is anything I've mentioned here especially difficult to obtain.

But thus armed, the *potential* forger is now prepared to become a *practicing* forger.

Chapter Three

Methods of Forgery: Alteration

Possibly the most convenient form of numismatic forgery involves the alteration of genuine, existing money. The advantages are certainly obvious, as a legitimate coin stands an excellent chance of being recognized as a legitimate coin, and only the alteration requires successful deception to be accepted. On the other hand, any modification of an actual coin must be as perfect in appearance as the rest of the coin. This requires extraordinary care.

There are four forms that numismatic forgery by alteration of coins may take:

1) *Tooling*

2) *Application*

3) *Embossing*

4) *Plating*

(Another term that is often heard — "defacing" — does not pertain to forgery.)

Tooling means exactly what it sounds like — the use of gravers, scrapers, files, blades, burnishers, and so forth to remove or rearrange certain detail on a coin's surface. Other than this and a magnifying glass, no special equipment is needed. Two things make tooling impractical, though. First, it is only feasible to create certain "coins" from certain other coins, greatly limiting the range of a forger's practice. Second, tooling can always be detected, and doesn't (or shouldn't) fool anyone anymore.

The heyday of tooling was during the 19th and early 20th century, a period when scores of 1801 silver dollars were converted into 1804s [1], and 1903 or 1910 Liberty nickels were tooled to resemble 1913s. There probably isn't one coin dealer out of ten who hasn't come across a "1914-

---

[1] This was especially a shame, since a number of very nice scarce, early dollars were thus mutilated in a senseless way that would fool no one today. (Even if the alteration had been done perfectly, genuine 1804 dollars were struck much later than 1804 and on different equipment; their fabric is completely unlike coins that were minted earlier.)

D" cent that was originally made in 1944, or a 1922 "plain" with a slight dimple where the mint mark it started out with used to be. The reason it has died out is simply that collectors have become better educated and grown more cautious than they were in the past. They are aware of which coins are susceptible to alteration by tooling in attempts to produce specific rarities, and they know just what differences — along with tooling marks — to check for. Today, any forger who naively tries to create such inadequate pieces should be looked upon as a pathetic amateur.

Photo of a genuine 1914-D Lincoln cent, shown next to an altered forgery made from a 1944-D. Note the difference in the spacing between the second and third numerals in the dates.

Application, in a sense, can be thought of as a process that is the opposite of tooling; instead of removing something from a coin's surface, something is added. Usually only a very minor (yet oh, how significant!) detail is involved, such as a mint mark. The most common way of doing this is to "shave" a mint mark from another coin, and then carefully glue or solder it in place. If done properly and with care, application can be very hard for the layman to detect.

Of gluing or soldering, gluing is by far the easiest. A good, free-flowing super glue (not gel) works best, and is invisible against the shiny background of an uncirculated coin. The shaved detail is carefully positioned on the coin's field, using the Optivisor and plenty of good light, and held gently in place with the point of a wooden toothpick. Next, a small drop of super glue is collected on the sharp end of a pin, and lightly touched to the edge of the detail being applied where it meets the field. Caution must be used to avoid touching the glue drop to the toothpick or the top of the detail; only the seam between the detail and the coin should receive the glue. This small gap will draw the liquid glue completely under the detail by capillary action. Any excess glue around the edge of the seam will remain liquid for only a minute or so, and must be removed immediately by carefully blotting with the edge of a facial tissue. The toothpick is lifted away, and the process is essentially complete.

Even this small amount of glue will act as a mask to oxidation, however, so the forger cannot apply toning or patina to the coin. Usually a forgery of this type will be stapled into a cardboard and cellophane coin holder before being offered for sale in an effort to prevent anything other than a visual inspection, since glued applications can easily be detected (and removed) with no damage to a coin by applying a drop of acetone or super glue solvent on a cotton swab to the suspicious area.

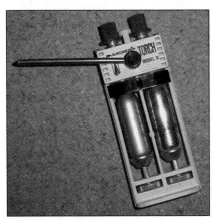

A needle torch, capable of pinpoint heat, is often the tool of choice for precision soldering applications. Care must be taken not to move the flame too close to the object being soldered.

Soldered applications are more difficult to do, but when they are done well they are also more difficult to detect. Just as with the glued application, the key to successful results is the use of a minimal amount of bonding material — except that with solder this is even more important, since any excess cannot be simply blotted away after the fact.

The coin is first supported by laying it upon its edges on top of a slightly open vise, so that heat from a small torch (propane, butane, or a needle torch) can be applied from below. (It is critical that the heat source come from the opposite side not only because this is how proper soldering is done, but because a shaved mint mark is so tiny that even the flame from a common match could melt it into a shapeless globule.) A small daub of paste flux (a little larger than the mint mark will be) is placed on the spot where the detail will be added, and then heat is slowly applied until the flux starts to "melt and spread". The heat is then quickly removed, and the coin allowed to cool.

Next a small chip of lead-free solder[2] — no more than about half the size of the mint mark itself — is positioned within the flux pool in the exact spot the detail will go. Heat is applied as before, until the solder chip suddenly forms a shiny sphere and then collapses into a "puddle". The heat is again removed, and as the coin begins to cool — but while it's still quite warm — a second small daub of paste flux is lightly touched to the solder, covering the solder with a thin, melted layer of the flux.

Now the mint mark can be gently placed atop the spot of solder. It will adhere to the flux, and need not be held down. The coin is heated a final time, and as the solder melts and puddles a second time it will "grab" the mint mark, forming a slight, curving meniscus between it and the flat field. The heat is immediately removed, and when the coin has cooled to the touch it is thoroughly cleaned of all flux residue with warm soapy water and cotton balls,[3] followed by a rinse.

The entire coin should now be plated to hide all traces of the solder. This step may seem obvious for coins made of copper or gold, but it is just as necessary for silver. A great many soldered applications have been detected because the forger, after all of his work and effort up to this point, suddenly got lazy and decided that the shiny surface of the solder looked enough like the rest of a silver coin to get by and not be noticed. It doesn't, and it won't, and it will be. A light electroplate is only a few molecules thick, and will in no way impair the detail or standards of a coin, yet it is enough to completely mask the solder and leave a perfectly uniform appearing surface. Toning or patina may then be applied right over the plate. Mint marks are the most common details added this way, but even numerals in dates are occasionally changed.

---

[2] Usually 95% tin/5% antimony, melts at about 430°F. Silver bearing solder may also be used (contains less than 2% silver, melts around 450°F.), but not "silver solder", which must use a brazing flux and melts at too high a temperature.

[3] To avoid causing scratches on the surface, one should never use anything more abrasive than a cotton ball when cleaning a coin.

When done with care, it can be extremely difficult for even an expert to detect a well-soldered application. But not always. I once saw a very nicely done "1964" Peace dollar that someone had created by first removing (tooling) the 3 from a 1934-D, then replacing it with a 6 that had been painstakingly shaved from a 1926. The soldered joint was remarkably smooth and clean, the plating was even, and the tooling marks were only faintly visible through a loupe. But it wasn't the tooling marks that gave this forgery away — it was the overall circulation wear (about EF-40) on a "coin" that should supposedly only exist in uncirculated condition![4]

Finally, there is also a rather extreme form of application that involves combining the entire obverse of one coin with the reverse of another. This can be accomplished one of three ways: poorly, cleverly, or brilliantly.

The simplest and poorest method is to merely remove one complete side of each coin and then solder the two halves together. The weakness of this method is the telltale solder seam around the edge of the forgery which can never be completely cleaned up or obscured, especially on a coin with a reeded edge. Modern coins struck in collars are perfectly round, their edges perpendicular, and the bottom of each and every serration on the edge has uniform, sharp corners. Any solder flowing from the center of the joined halves must extend to the edge, and would unavoidably seep slightly over, softening detail that should be crisp. A more clever way is to leave the entire edge and rim of one of the coins intact, fitting the face of the second coin inside of it, the same way a lid fits into the rim of a jar.

The forger begins by turning a pair of mandrels out of aluminum on his lathe, which will be used for holding the coins as he works on them. (These mandrels resemble, more than anything else, oversized thumbtacks with thick shafts and heads. The "head" is turned to be perfectly flat on its outward face, and is of slightly greater diameter than the coin. The shaft is the portion that is held by the jaws of the lathe chuck. Since the rim of a coin is the highest part of its detail, a coin placed upon the face of one of these mandrels will lie absolutely flat.) The side of each coin which is to be saved now receives a drop of super glue and is attached to a mandrel, leaving the unwanted side facing outward.

---

4 The Denver mint struck 316,076 silver Peace dollars dated 1964, but none were ever released into circulation. All were ordered melted down. There have been rumors for years that a specimen or two may have survived this melt, but if so none has ever been reported, and the idea of one actually having circulated is patently ridiculous.

Fixing the first mandrel in the lathe, the jaws of the chuck are adjusted until the coin is perfectly centered. The forger now machines out the entire center of the coin to half its thickness, right up to the inside edge of the rim (the point where the rim drops down to meet the coin's field). This mandrel is now removed from the lathe and the next one set up and centered. On this second coin the first step is to remove the entire outside rim for the full thickness of the coin, leaving a rimless coin of exactly the same diameter as the cavity in the first coin. Next the unwanted face is machined off so that the remainder is again half its original thickness.

The forger checks the fit of the two halves, and if satisfactory, removes the second mandrel from the lathe. A soak in super glue solvent will release the both coin halves from the mandrels. The face of the second coin should fit cleanly into the rim of the first, with the seam joining the two running along the inside edge if the rim.

The halves are now either glued or soldered together, using similar methods to those described earlier. Soldering is again better, as the slight meniscus formed by the flow around the seam will fill in the hairline gap. The tricky part is to use just the right amount of solder to complete the joint but not overflow it. Afterward, of course, the coin must be plated.

A slight modification of this technique, which I consider to be brilliant, is to make both the coin face which is to fit inside the rim, and the corresponding space to receive it, just slightly larger in diameter than the example just described. This will cause the seam to lie upon a point midway along the thin width of the rim. Once the halves are joined, evidence of this seam is then flawlessly obliterated by lightly burnishing[5] the rim along this line.

Embossing describes the process of employing a small partial die (containing only a mint mark on a small area of flat field) and pushing the coin's metal up into the die space to add detail. This type of alteration is virtually undetectable at the altered site, because the added mint mark was created in exactly the same way that a genuine mint mark is produced. The disadvantage, however, is that since the metal must be pushed outward from inside the coin, a hole has to be made somewhere on the coin to get inside. This entry hole will then have to be filled in and the coin's surface restored, which will always leave detectable traces of

---

[5] Burnishing, by the way, is simply polishing or smoothing a piece of metal by rubbing it with another smooth piece of metal.

tooling marks. The method is still a very effective one, though, probably because on a coin that is valued for its having a mint mark, most people will examine with care only the area of the mint mark itself in order to try to determine whether or not it was actually raised in a die as part of the coin. In the case of an embossed alteration, that is exactly what has happened. This process is still so new and uncommon that few people think of looking for evidence of alteration elsewhere.

Raising a mint mark by embossing is normally accomplished by entering the coin either from its edge, or from a point on the side directly opposite from where the mint mark will appear.

For entry to be practical from the edge, three very important conditions must exist. First, the coin must have a plain edge. It is difficult enough to attempt to restore the perfectly round contour of a coin with a plain edge without leaving at least some evidence of tooling, but it is impossible to restore a reeded edge. Second, the coin must be thick enough to allow a hole large enough to admit the portion of the embossing tool that will push the coin's metal outward. And third, the normal location of the coin's mint mark must be very near the edge of the coin's field. All of these conditions are met in the case of the Buffalo nickel; it is the thickest U.S. coin with a plain edge, and its mint mark is just inside the rim on its reverse. As a matter of fact, the embossing technique was probably devised specifically for this coin, as the first examples started turning up just several years ago, causing quite a bit of excitement in numismatic circles at the time. As I recall, nickels dated 1926 were discovered having been embossed with either a D or an S.

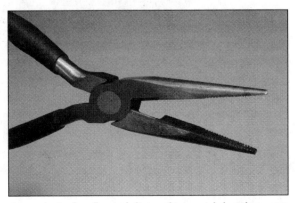

A normal pair of needle-nosed pliers, nothing special about them — yet.

A specialized tool had to be developed in order to do this embossing — basically a modified pair of long-nosed pliers. The tips of the pliers jaws are first heated with a torch until they are red hot, then bent inwards about a quarter inch from the ends at a 90° angle, so that the tips will close against each other. After cooling slowly (which will also anneal the metal and make it workable), the tip of one of these jaws (we will call it the upper jaw from now on) is filed nice and smooth,[6] so that the mint mark can be stamped or engraved upon it, forming the "die". If the forger possesses a set of tiny little letter stamps, with serifs, that read in reverse for most letter stamp sets, then he is all set; otherwise he will have to engrave the mint mark.

This is actually much easier to do than it sounds. Using a simple pantograph with its reducing tracer consisting of a tool steel rod (old broken drill bit) sharpened to a 60° cone, a comfortably oversized pattern will allow just about anyone to produce a perfectly credible mint mark impression in a die. Here the Optivisor will definitely come in handy. Also, as with the hand engraving of any die, the work is checked continually by lightly pressing a piece of soft lead against it as it progresses. When the image on the lead comes out looking perfect, the die is finished.

A pantograph being used to trace over a master pattern to cut a mintmark on an embossing tool (half of a pair of needle-nose pliers).

---

[6] The field of a Buffalo nickel slopes upward slightly toward the rim, so the face of this die must be contoured to fit it.

With the upper jaw all taken care of, the lower jaw is ready to be ground, filed, and shaped until it resembles a short rod protruding from the tapering end of the jaw, with a small, rounded "lump" sitting on top of the very end of it. (This rod should be capable of entering a 1/16" hole to a depth of 1/8".) When the pliers are closed, this lump should touch the dead center of the mint mark image on the upper jaw. The completed tool is tested by embossing a thin piece of lead, and if the lump on the end of the rod can easily push the metal up into the die, it is hardened, tempered, and ready to use on a coin.

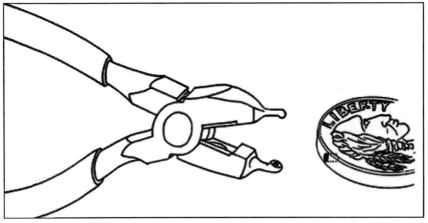

Jaws of needle-nosed pliers adapted to emboss a mint mark onto a coin from its edge.

A 1/16" diameter hole is carefully drilled about 3/16" deep into the edge of the Buffalo nickel, at a point that lies directly between the E and the C in the words FIVE CENTS on the reverse. The tool is inserted, positioned, pressed lightly (it takes very little pressure to raise detail as small as a mint mark), and removed. The entry hole is now filled with solder, and the surface of the coin's edge carefully restored.

The only major drawback to this procedure — aside from the possibility of leaving tool marks while smoothing the edge — is that the solder cannot be successfully hidden simply by nickel plating the entire coin. Nickel plating is usually done with pure nickel, which has a distinctly different tone from the 25% nickel/75% copper alloy used for the U.S. five cent piece. (This is how the first embossed nickels I mentioned earlier were eventually discovered — by the solder spot on the coin's edge.) It is possible, however, to insulate both faces of the coin with varnish (removed afterward with solvent) and plate only the edge of the coin with pure nickel, which will be less noticeable than an overall plate.

But the Buffalo nickel is certainly not the only coin vulnerable to alteration by embossing. By slightly modifying the design of the lower jaw of the embossing tool so that it resembles a thin, upright rod, mint marks may be easily applied much further away from the rim of a coin than is possible by drilling in from the edge. This also means that coins with reeded edges can be successfully embossed.

To do this requires that the entry hole be made on one of the faces of the coin, at the exact spot opposite where the mint mark will appear on the other side. Since obviously the hole will have to be filled and the coin's surface restored, coin types that lend themselves to this treatment are limited to those where the hole will fall on easy to blend detail — not upon a flat field, complex detail, or lettering, all of which is difficult to simulate. Good candidates would be the silver Washington quarter, where this hole would be on the smooth outer curve of the hair at the top of the head, or the silver Roosevelt dime (the forehead just in front of the hairline).

There are several others where this alignment works out, as well.

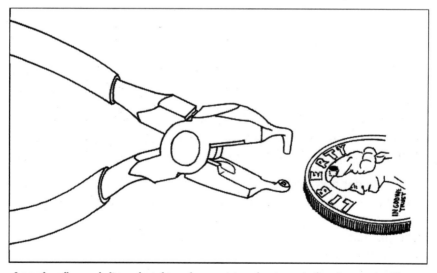

Jaws of needle-nosed pliers adapted to emboss a mint mark onto a coin from its opposite side.

Since the tool will be entering the coin straight through the side, rather than upward from the edge, the hole need be no larger than the mint mark itself, or about 1/32", making the amount of tooling required to restore the surface quite minimal. The hole is drilled to a depth of half to three-fourths the thickness of the coin, and the tool is applied, pressed, and withdrawn. Once the hole is filled and smoothed, either the entire coin or just the side that was repaired is plated. This type of alteration, done well, is very difficult to detect.

But we're not quite ready to move on yet. Just as there was with application, there is also a final form of embossing to discuss. This last method uses no special tool, and requires no distortion, soldering, restoration, or plating of the coin's surface. It does not affect the coin's weight, tone, specific gravity, or spectrographic analysis. It can be used on any coin of any denomination made of any alloy, and it leaves absolutely no trace whatsoever.

I ask you to imagine, if you will, what would happen if it were possible to take a coin that was originally struck without a mint mark and *return* it — just for a moment — to the *exact same* dies that produced it, the only difference being that this time a mint mark has been added to one of the dies. With a very slight amount of pressure — no more than a light hammer tap, really — enough stress could be induced through the entire coin at once to cause the minute amount of metal necessary to fill the mint mark to displace itself and do so.

But it isn't possible for a forger to obtain the original dies for a coin, you say? Well, of course it isn't. But it *is* possible to *create* perfect dies for any coin, from any coin. Keep this idea in mind for the time being, and I'll show you how the dies can be made a bit later on.

Plating is the last form of numismatic forgery by alteration, and it is far more successful than application, though less common. In fact, like the final form of embossing I just mentioned, it is undetectable.

But first, let's clear something up. Alteration by plating does not mean applying a full electroplate layer to the entire surface of a coin — as when covering evidence of soldering — in order to try to make a coin look like it is made of something else!

For instance, everybody knows that in 1943 the United States struck cents made of zinc-plated steel, not the usual solid bronze alloy. Everybody also knows that a few bronze planchets left over from 1942 accidentally got mixed in on the first day of minting, and that ever since then the "copper 1943 cent" has been a great rarity. Everybody also knows that a copper plated steel cent is still a steel cent, and will stick to a magnet regardless of its color. Only an idiot would attempt to offer such an obvious fraud as a forgery, and only a greater idiot would be taken in by it. (I'll show you how easy it is to manufacture a bronze 1943 cent that is actually made of bronze a little later, when we discuss *hubbing* and the *brockage principle*.)

Similarly, almost everybody is aware that in 1883, when Liberty nickels were first introduced, the government did not include the word "CENTS" anywhere on the coin, and that enterprising people immediately began gold plating the still unfamiliar coins and passing them off as five-dollar gold pieces. (The word "CENTS" was added to a hastily revised reverse within a matter of weeks.) Such contemporary gold plated alterations were actually *counterfeits* — not forgeries — and there is certainly no current market for forgeries of counterfeits!

What alteration by plating *does* mean is the building up of a small area of detail (like a mint mark) by selectively masking every other part of a coin, so that only the area left exposed will receive the plate. By allowing the current to flow for a longer period of time than for the plating examples we have discussed thus far, a thick enough plate can be deposited to actually "grow" a mint mark right on the surface of the coin.[7]

The trickiest part to doing this is being able to get the mint mark to come out looking professionally done. Obviously this cannot be achieved by simply attempting to scratch the outline of the detail freehand through a layer of insulating varnish with a pin! Just as a larger pattern could be neatly miniaturized onto the jaw of an embossing tool by using a pantograph, the forger can easily lay out a perfectly formed mint mark by working from an oversized pattern. But instead of using a pantograph, which would scratch a gouge into the very part of the coin he wishes to build up, he will use photography.

---

[7] This technique was revealed to me by the forger Mark Hofmann during one of my interviews with him at the Utah State Prison in 1987. While Mark went on to gain notoriety as a master document forger, he actually began with numismatics. His very first forgery (at age 14) was to add a mint mark to an uncirculated silver dollar using the plating method described here. He bragged that the coin was subsequently certified by ANACS (American Numismatic Association Certification Service) as authentic.

The process is not unlike preparing blank circuit boards for photo etching. "Printed" circuit boards are actually created by photographically imprinting the desired designs, circuits, and so forth from a negative onto a sheet of metal-covered circuit board that has been treated with a light-sensitive emulsion. This board is then "developed", leaving a masked/unmasked surface, which is etched with an acid to produce the circuit board. On a coin, of course, the forger will not be using an etchant to *remove* metal, but a plating solution and electrical current to *add* it.

He begins by inspecting and measuring an appropriate genuine mint mark, and then prepares a suitably enlarged drawing of it in a scale that will lend itself easily to reduction. Eight times the original size is fairly easy to work with, and would be reduced to 12.5%.

The main thing the forger needs to be aware of at this point is that everything that appears black on his drawing will eventually end up as a mask film on the coin's surface, so he will want to draw a *white* mint mark against a *black* background. From this drawing a high-contrast "litho" negative can easily be made by any commercial lithographic service[8] in the proper reduced size. On this finished negative the black background from the drawing will be clear, while the mint mark detail will appear as a tiny black letter.

The next step involves photo sensitizing the coin where the mint mark will be added. This is done by brushing a small, even amount of a chemical known as *photo resist* (available at any electronics supply store, along with developer) on the coin. Since photo resist is light sensitive, the forger will have to work with this chemical and the sensitized coin in subdued lighting conditions, and it is best if the coin is kept in the dark as it dries (24 hours).

The negative is now fitted to the coin directly over this sensitized area, trimming the edges around the mint mark so that it can lie flat against the field. It is important that the emulsion (dull) side if the negative be in contact with the coin's surface in order to produce a clean, crisp image. The forger holds the negative in place with a small strip of clear tape, and exposes the coin to a strong ultraviolet light source, such as the sun or a photocopying machine. The negative can now be removed and the image on the coin

---

[8] I imagine that a sensible forger, having a negative made elsewhere, would probably want to camouflage his real intent by incorporating his mint mark drawing into something innocuous — like a larger pattern for an ordinary circuit board (a routine and unmemorable job for most lithographic services.)

developed, using the developer solution recommended for whichever brand of photo resist the forger has used. Once this developing has taken place, followed by a water rinse, the coin may again be handled in normal light.

If the forger has done everything properly up to this point (and the whole procedure is really so simple that it would be difficult to foul it up) he will have a coin with a spot of masking film covering the mint mark area, with a perfect mint mark-shaped opening in it right where he wants it to be. It is now a straightforward matter to apply a coat of insulating varnish to the rest of the coin — front, back, and edge — thoroughly covering every part of it except for the mint mark opening and a tiny spot on the rim, where the clip at the end of the wire running from the power source will be attached.

In electroplating, the object receiving the plate is attached to the positive terminal of a very weak (usually about one volt) DC power source, forming a *cathode*. The *anode*, which is connected to the negative terminal, is composed of a strip of the metal being used to plate. When both are suspended in an acidic plating solution, an electrical circuit is formed which actually detaches molecules from the surface of the anode, draws them through the solution, and deposits them on the cathode.

Alteration by plating is especially suitable for uncirculated coins of gold or silver, as the surface of the plate resembles mint luster even under a loupe. Copper plate is somewhat reddish and off-color by comparison, and cannot produce a mint luster unless it has actually been struck; it may, however, be successfully toned.

The advantages of creating numismatic forgeries by altering existing coins are often outweighed by a very singular disadvantage — that of the forger's greed. To alter existing coins requires first the acquisition of existing coins, which is not only an expense in itself, but also places a limitation on the amount of forgery that can be done. Moreover, each alteration is unique, and thus requires individualized attention and a notable investment of time and effort.

Though some forgers seem to specialize in alterations only, quite a few become attracted to the higher volume potential of creating entire coins. There are basically only two ways to do this: by casting, or by striking with dies.

Chapter Four

Methods of Forgery: Casting

While decidedly not the best way to produce an accurate copy of most coins, casting is very likely the oldest method known, and remains one of the easiest. The reason it isn't as common these days as it once was is that even under the best of conditions there are so many pitfalls and potential errors inherent to it. If these are not known and carefully coped with, they will most certainly create evidence that will lead to detection. Still, if proper care is taken and the forger is willing to work within the limitations of what the process is capable of, some very convincing (though not absolutely undetectable) forgeries can be produced by casting them.

The greatest advantage the casting process has to offer is the totally faithful duplication of detail from the original master. All the devices on a coin's surface, regardless of how simple or how intricate, are reproduced from the mold exactly as they should be, with never the slightest variation. A portrait or an eagle or a wreath on a cast coin has exactly the same look as its counterpart it was taken from. And this detail is not only properly laid out and proportioned, but with modern pressure casting made possible by the use of a centrifuge, it can be incredibly sharp.

There is a jeweler in my community who displays in his store a rose that he invested in plaster, burned out, and cast in gold. (Gold, because of its mass and density, has probably the greatest flow property of any molten metal used for casting.) Every petal on this rose, every pistil and stamen, every leaf and thorn, was perfectly captured — but so was something else. Unnoticed by the jeweler, a single aphid was standing on the stem of one of the leaves at the moment the flower was covered with plaster. Trapped, the aphid clung to the stem as the investment hardened, and was reduced to ash as the mold was fired. When the gold flowed into the mold, the tiny holes left by the aphid's hair-like legs served as sprues to carry the metal into the cavity left by its body, creating a perfect, solid gold aphid smaller than the head of a pin. Under magnification, it is possible to see even the parasites attached to the body of this gold aphid!

But while casting can produce such amazing detail as this, it has certain disadvantages, as well. Some can be overcome to a degree, some cannot.

For one thing, the metal in a cast coin is less dense than in a die struck coin. Striking with dies during minting is actually a form of "cold forging" which compresses a genuine coin's metal, making it harder than it was originally. A cast coin, having solidified from molten metal, is soft, loose, and "spongy" by comparison. This difference is not discernable by visual inspection, but the two types, spun on a hard table top, will "ring" differently.

The casting process is also susceptible to numerous conditions which could cause surface flaws on the finished cast: air bubbles caught in the investment along the surface of the cavity, mold seams on the edge of the wax model, the sprue attachment location — all require repair, which will leave at least some evidence of tooling marks. The metal could be too hot when injected (causing voids), or too cool (laminations), or carry slag with it (inclusions).

The most persistent problem with casting, however, is *differential shrinkage*. Any elementary physics class will tell us that heat makes an object expand; common sense should tell us that if an object becomes solid when it is hot, it will have to contract as it cools. This is just what happens with a cast. If a forger were to prepare a mold using a silver dollar model made of wax that was the exact, correct size in every dimension that it ought to be, his finished cast in silver would be between two to three percent smaller in diameter, while the center of the coin could be as much as twenty percent thinner than the original coin.

Efforts can be made to attempt to create an oversize mold to compensate for differential shrinkage, but it will be next to impossible to consistently duplicate the exacting standards typical of modern coinage.[1] Frankly, I have never seen or heard of a successful (undetectable to a layman) cast forgery of any modern coin.

In order to minimize the measurable effects of differential shrinkage, the forger will have to avoid trying to cast anything that is supposed to be thin, flat, and of precise weight and diameter. This leaves him with the alternative of casting objects that are thick, globular, and at least moderately variable — terms which aptly describe most types of ancient

---

[1] When you think about it, by the way, this is the main reason modern coinage evolved about two hundred years ago — to make counterfeiting as difficult as possible.

coinage. It shouldn't surprise us, then, to learn that most cast forgeries are of ancients, and that most forgeries of ancients are cast.

But a casting can turn out no better than the master it is based upon, so the forger's first concern is to choose a high quality original to copy. The surface of this master coin must be as clean as possible — right down to the metal — without any corrosion, pitting, or crust-like build up of hard patina. There should be no serious cuts, scratches, marks, gouges, flan cracks, or laminations that would distinguish the coin, and any wear should be even and consistent overall.

Once the forger is satisfied with the condition of both sides, he turns his attention to the coin's edge. The planchets most ancient coins were struck from have a thickly rounded, irregular, somewhat lumpy-looking edge to them, the result of both how they were originally prepared and the minting process that was used. The forger is looking for the part of the edge with the least surface detail to it, for this is where he will attach the sprue. This spot will be the only part of the finished cast that will have to be cleaned up and smoothed over by tooling.

From this point on, producing a numismatic forgery by centrifugal casting is a straightforward process involving just six basic steps:

1. Rubber Mold From Master

One end of a short piece of 1/8" brass rod (about 3/4" long) is attached with a drop of super glue to the edge of the coin serving as the master, so that it resembles a small lollipop. This rod will support the coin in a form as the mold is being made, and serve as a master for the sprue channel at the same time.

The form into which the mold rubber is poured is simplicity itself. All it consists of is a strip of 3/4" wide sheet brass (of the sort commonly available at hobby stores) about 8 inches long with the ends bent upwards at right angles on either side, so that it looks like a square-cornered letter "U" about the size of a deck of cards. Right in the center of the inside bottom of this "U" is soldered a small hemispherical base, about a half inch in diameter, with a 1/8" hole drilled into it. (The "stem" of the coin "lollipop" goes in this socket.) The form is sandwiched between two small panes of glass and held together with a rubber band, and it's ready to use.

RTV silicone, a self-vulcanizing, pourable rubber consisting of a base and catalyst mixture that cures at room temperature, is used to make the mold. Several varieties are available from different manufacturers, so it is worthwhile for the forger to research the properties and characteristics of each, and choose one that is best suited to his needs. Product data sheets (available from distributors) normally provide information about such things as working time, rate of cure, tear strength, elongation, shrinkage, compatibility with other materials, inhibitors, and so forth. For example, some RTVs are rated at .1 or .2% shrinkage after seven days, while others are rated 0%, and still others "nil".[2] Since a forger has to accept some amount of differential shrinkage in his final casting anyway, it would make sense to avoid introducing any additional shrinkage along the way that could be prevented.

A product I've always had very good results with is Dow's Silastic-E RTV Silicone Rubber. I mix it in a paper cup with a popsicle stick in a ratio of one part catalyst to ten parts base by weight (some leeway is allowed) and come up with a pourable liquid of about the same consistency as latex paint. It can be poured directly into the mold form (containing the coin!) this way after mixing, but it is better to first expose the mixture to a vacuum of 26"-29" of mercury for 3-5 minutes to eliminate the tiny air bubbles throughout it that were formed by stirring. This precaution will in turn prevent the chance of surface "dimples" occurring on the wax models.[3]

After fully curing (usually about 24 hours) the mold can be removed from the form. The forger now has a block of rubber with a valuable coin stuck inside of it, neither of which is doing him much good at the moment. The mold will have to be "opened" in order to remove the master and to be able to use the mold. He does this by carefully slicing the mold in half (thickness-wise) with a single-edged razor blade, making sure that the rubber splits cleanly to form a seam along the edge of the coin and the sprue channel inside. The surfaces produced by this cut do not have to be perfectly flat — in fact, it will help to keep the halves properly aligned when the mold is in use if they are somewhat irregular.[4]

---

[2] I haven't been able to figure out what the difference is supposed to be between "0%" and "nil", but I have seen both terms used by the same manufacturer for different RTVs in their product line.

[3] If a bubble of air in the rubber is present near the surface of the mold cavity, the hot wax filling the mold can cause the air in the bubble to expand slightly, pushing a small part of the mold inward and causing a "dimple" to form on the surface of the wax as it solidifies. This feature is then passed on to the final casting, and becomes a factor that can lead to detection.

[4] Many jewelers, when making a mold like this, routinely "corrugate" all four corners to guarantee a perfect alignment.

An RTV rubber mold after being cut apart, releasing the master. Note the corrugated corners, which assist in aligning the mold halves when they are assembled.

The mold is now finished, and can be used to produce as many wax models as the forger wishes.

2. Wax Model From Mold

A special type of wax known as "injection wax" (available from jewelry manufacturing supply sources) must be used with this kind of mold. As with RTV rubbers, there are many different kinds with varying properties to choose from. Some are rather brittle, others more flexible; some experience quite a bit of differential shrinkage as they cool, while others have hardly any at all. The things a forger will want to look for are flexibility (to help prevent breakage), "readability" (the degree to which detail stands out clearly to the eye), and, of course, as little shrinkage as possible. Also, some injection waxes work best when a release agent is used on the mold, but the forger should avoid these. An easy release wax that does not require such an agent will pull much sharper detail.

The best way to set up the mold for use is to take advantage of the smooth, perfectly flat outer sides that were created by contact with the glass panes of the mold form. Those same panes are used to support the mold by lightly dampening one side of each and pressing the smooth side of a mold half to it. Surface tension will hold the rubber firmly to the glass, providing a rigid, distortion-free mounting. The halves are then assembled and held together with — that's right, a rubber band.

Melted wax is injected into the mold through the sprue channel opening. Professional jewelers often use a commercially made injection pot, which is like an electric crock pot with a spigot and a small pump. These are nice, and the temperature of the wax can be controlled very accurately, but unless a great deal of wax injection is being done all at once, they aren't really necessary. Equally good results can be had by melting the wax in a small sauce pan on the kitchen stove, and injecting it with a 10cc glass veterinary syringe (minus the hypodermic needle). When the wax cools, the mold is taken apart and the model can be removed and inspected. Occasionally there will be a void or two on the edge where air was trapped in the mold, but this can easily be remedied by cutting small channels in the rubber for the air to escape.

Investment wax being injected into a mold, with finished wax models. This particular coin, an 1858 fifty-cent piece, is not suitable for producing a convincing forgery by casting due to the problems encountered by differential shrinkage.

The edge of the model may show a fine parting line from the seam between the two mold halves. This should be eliminated before the wax is invested, otherwise it will show up on the final cast, and it will be much more difficult to remove then. The forger can do this by moving a hot wire next to (not touching) the wax along this line, allowing its radiant heat to lightly melt the surface of the wax. Now the model, with its wax sprue still attached, is ready to invest.

A well made mold will produce wax images faithful in every detail to the original coin.

3. Investing the Wax Model

Just as the first mold was produced by surrounding a master coin with RTV rubber, this second mold is made by embedding the wax model in investment plaster. It is this plaster mold that will be used to cast the actual forged coin. Most of the effort involved with this step has to do with proper preparation of the form used to hold the investment.

Commercially made investment forms and bases are available, but I've never found that their expense justifies their use, especially for smaller amounts of work. Homemade forms are just as easy to use, work just as well, are much cheaper, and — as added incentive to the furtive forger, leave no record of their acquisition or clues as to their use.

A base is easily made by sawing a 6" X 6" square from a piece of masonite (or plywood, or particle board, or just about anything flat and smooth). Onto this base a puddle of melted beeswax is poured, forming a circle that will be about 1/2" greater in diameter than the finished mold, and about 1/8" thick. The flame of a small torch is lightly flicked across the surface of the puddle until it is smooth, and the wax is allowed to cool. Next a small lump of soft beeswax, about half the size of a walnut, is formed into a cone and pressed into the center of the puddle. It is quite important that the base of this cone forms a perfectly smooth transition to the flat surface around it, because this is the very spot where molten metal will be thrown into the mold with a good deal of force by the centrifuge. Any folds, cracks, or rough areas on the wax will become filled with plaster, which will create fragile and unnecessary areas on the mold that could break off and produce inclusions in the cast. The seam can be contoured and blended with the end of a blunt rod, and then smoothed with a few gentle flicks from a flame. A 1/8" rod is now pressed into the top of this cone, creating a socket for the sprue of the wax model.

With the wax model set into this socket, the joint between the sprue and the top of the cone must also be blended and made completely smooth. Using a flame now could damage the detail on the model, so a hot wire is applied the same way it was used earlier to eliminate the parting line on the edge of the model.

Another part of the investment form will also become the outside shell of the finished mold. All it consists of is a piece of large diameter steel tubing (similar to industrial electrical conduit) cut to the desired length. The inside diameter should allow at least 1/2" clearance from the side to the nearest part of the wax model, and its length should extend from the base to about 1" above the model's highest point. The tubing is centered over the cone on the base, and pressed into the soft wax. (Note — a better seal can be obtained if the tubing is first heated just enough to be unpleasant to touch, and then pressed into the wax.) With the form now ready, the forger may mix and pour his investment.

This is a good place to try to dispel, if I may, a certain prevalent myth about lost wax casting: *Ordinary, over-the-counter plaster of Paris is NEVER used as investment!* I can't begin to guess how many times I've come across some cursory treatment of the subject and read a phrase like, ". . . the wax model is then covered with plaster of Paris, *et cetera, et cetera . . .*" Every single time this sort of statement has been just plain *wrong*. The microscopic particles which make up plaster of Paris are much larger and coarser than those of a proper investment plaster, and their bond behaves radically different under conditions of high heat. *If* it were possible to burn the wax out of a mold made of plaster of Paris without it exploding all over the oven (and it isn't), the thing would shatter as soon as the molten metal from the centrifuge touched it. Investment plaster is specially formulated to withstand the high temperatures encountered during the casting process, while ordinary plaster of Paris is not.

What this means to the forger is that he will need to obtain his investment plaster from a jewelry manufacturing supply source, the same as he did with his injection wax. Certain trade names like *Crystobolite* or *Satin Cast* are often used, but the generic term is simply *investment*.

When properly mixed, investment should have about the same consistency as watery yogurt. In other words, a spoonful ought to be able to maintain a heaping, rounded shape when it is held still, but when the handle of the spoon is tapped with a pencil the mound of plaster should begin to collapse and settle. Similar to plaster of Paris, the forger will only have about fifteen minutes to work with mixed investment before it begins to set up.

Mixing, of course, requires stirring, which introduces air, which causes bubbles. Since the mixture is so thick, it is difficult for these small air bubbles that are scattered all throughout the investment to rise to the surface. Unless they are removed many will still be present when the plaster sets up, and this can result in serious blemishes on the cast.

For instance, if a slowly rising bubble should come into contact with the model, it will have a tendency to cling. (Drop a coin into a glass of carbonated soft drink some time and watch what happens.) This is especially likely if a bubble becomes caught in deep detail such as lettering, hair curls, and so forth. When the investment sets, these clinging bubbles will become voids in the mold which will be filled in by molten metal, leaving bumpy globs on the surface of the final cast that are impossible to remove or clean up. Even if an air bubble is only trapped *near* the model, but not quite actually touching it, the pressure of the flowing metal may break through the ultra-thin layer of plaster separating the two, connecting it to the mold cavity with a pinhole-sized "sprue". The resulting cast will show a tiny sphere resting on the coin's surface, which may or may not be removable without leaving obvious traces.

But the forger can easily avoid such problems by removing the bubbles from his investment. Using a vacuum table exactly the same way as described earlier for the RTV mixture, all of the air can also be cleared from wet plaster. Lacking a vacuum table, the container of mixed investment can be vibrated for a few minutes by holding it up against an electric motor tool, such as a bench grinder. This is a fairly effective means of forcing most of the air bubbles in the mixture to rise. There is also a surface tension relieving agent known as "de-bubble solution" (basically soapy water and alcohol) which can be sprayed on the wax model and allowed to dry before the investment is poured. This will help discourage bubbles from clinging, but it does nothing to prevent them from occurring nearby. Another time honored method is to use a soft-bristled watercolor brush to "paint" a layer of bubble-free investment onto the model, building up a layer about an eighth of an inch thick. (This is an excellent way to visually assure that all detail is completely filled in.) When this shell has just barely begun to set up — but while the surface still has some tack — a fresh batch of investment is poured into the mold form, covering it. Bubbles in this second batch won't matter, because the bubble-free coating around the model is thick enough to prevent flaws.

After the mold has set up and cured for 24 hours[5] it is removed from the base and the wax is ready to be burned out. Casting is always done immediately following burn out while the mold is still hot, so if for any reason the forger doesn't wish to cast soon after pouring the mold, he can save it by placing it in a plastic bag to prevent it from drying out too much. A mold kept this way should be used within a couple of weeks.

4. Burn Out Wax

Here is where the term "lost wax" derives from. When the mold is turned upside-down and heated, the wax melts and runs out through the sprue channel, leaving behind the cavity into which the molten metal is injected. If it sounds simple, it's because it really is. But there is just a little bit more to it than this, though, if it is to be done right.

With the sprue opening facing down, the investment mold is placed in the center of the bake-out oven, resting atop a ceramic trivet (or three small ceramic blocks) so that it stands about half an inch off from the floor of the kiln. The forger must check to be sure that he has ample room to be able to grasp the mold with tongs when the burn out is completed, and also that he has enough space at the front of the oven to set the centrifuge crucible when it is time to begin its pre-heating.

---

[5] Some investments require as little as eight hours. Moisture remaining in the investment will not have an adverse effect.

The pyrometer control on the side of the kiln is set to slowly raise the temperature to 500° Fahrenheit, where it is held for about an hour. There will be a considerable amount of smoke from the melted, burning wax coming from the vent hole on top of the oven, so the forger needs to have a small evacuating fan overhead.

When the kiln stops smoking, it means that all of the wax has been burned off. The crucible must be properly pre-heated for a quality casting, so it is now set inside next to the mold. The temperature is raised to 1250° F., which will usually take about another thirty minutes. Once this temperature is reached, the forger is ready to make his cast.

5. Operating the Centrifuge

Using a metal casting centrifuge is just like acquiring any new skill; it can be a little tricky at first, but it's also pretty easy once a person gets the hang of it. The whole secret is to be systematic about the procedure. Time is of the essence. The forger has to develop confident, practiced movements that flow logically and naturally from each step to the next.

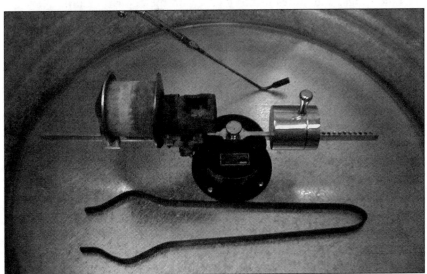

Principal parts of a centrifuge: On center arm, left to right — lock at rear of mold; mold form containing investment (from which wax has been melted out, or "lost"); crucible in holder; center pivot on spring-wound base and rotating arm lock; counterweight set to balance center arm; handle for winding and releasing arm. Top — oxy-acetylene torch with flood heat tip. Bottom — tongs for handling mold form and crucible. The entire apparatus is mounted in a galvanized steel tub to prevent accidental fire or loss of spilled precious metal.

The first thing the forger must do is balance the centrifuge arm. As soon as the investment mold is finished — but *before* it is burned out — it is mounted in place at the far end of one side of the arm, just in front of the crucible. The mouth of the crucible should line up with and empty directly into the sprue opening on the mold. With the mold and crucible in place, the counterweight on the opposite end of the arm is moved and adjusted so that the entire arm balances evenly on its center pivot.

This center point is set into a spring wound base. To ready the centrifuge for use, the arm is given four or five complete turns clockwise against the pressure of the spring, and then held in place by moving a small locking slide on the base outward to rest against a lug protruding from the arm to prevent it from spinning. The mold can now be removed and burned out, and the crucible pre-heated.

When the bake-out oven reaches 1250° F., the door is opened. At this temperature both the crucible and the mold will be glowing red — but this won't last for long. As soon as they are removed from the oven their temperature will start to drop at the rate of about a hundred degrees a minute, so the forger must work quickly. He removes first the crucible with the tongs, and slides it into its rack on the centrifuge arm. Next he takes out the mold and carefully positions and locks it into place. By the time the forger has placed his casting metal into the crucible and lighted his oxy-acetylene torch (with the flood heating tip), the outside metal tubing on the mold will have cooled to a dull, scaly gray, while the cavity within the mold will still be glowing red. This is just right.

The flame from the torch is played upon the metal in the crucible.[6] As it begins to melt and flow, a pinch of dry granular brazing flux is added to prevent oxide formation.[7] The flame is continued so that all of the metal in the crucible is completely melted, and has the appearance of a glowing, flowing globule with a swirling surface. Too much heat and delay at this point could boil the metal, causing voids to occur in the cast, so the forger must now work very quickly.

Keeping the flame on the metal right up until the last possible moment, the forger takes hold of the counterweight end of the centrifuge arm and

[6] The metals a forger will use for this process will invariably be an alloy of either gold, silver, or bronze/brass, all of which have melting points within about a hundred degrees of 1800° F. The finest results with the greatest detail and least differential shrinkage are obtained with gold, followed by silver, followed by bronze/brass.

[7] Since it does not tarnish or oxidize, some jewelers do not use any flux when casting gold. I have found that it never hurts, though, and that with any molten metal flux helps to keep alloys in solution.

turns it a further quarter turn clockwise. This operates a cam on the center pivot which withdraws the locking slide back into the base. He then simultaneously lifts his flame and releases the arm. The centrifuge will spin rapidly, throwing the molten metal from the crucible deep into the hot mold, filling every crevice of the cavity with great pressure. This metal will begin to cool and solidify almost immediately, so that by the time the centrifuge begins to slow down the casting will be complete.

If the forger has used the proper amount of metal for the cast, the sprue channel and entry cone on the face of the mold will be completely filled. The extra weight of this bit of molten metal helps significantly to increase the pressure — and hence improve the detail — on the casting in the cavity. The mold can now be removed from the centrifuge (using tongs — it is still quite hot!) and set aside to cool.

6. Treatment of Cast

The safest way to remove the cast from the plaster is to place the entire mold in a bucket of water and allow it to soak for several hours. Burned investment plaster is quite porous, and will literally fall apart after absorbing enough water. The finished casting, sprue still attached, is easily located by groping through the plaster sludge at the bottom of the bucket. After rinsing it off, it can be properly inspected.

If the forger has done everything well, he should have an elegantly detailed facsimile of the original master coin, with no surface dimples, bubbles, seams, or other visible flaws. Its finished diameter and weight will be slightly less than the original master (due to differential shrinkage), but this effect will be minimized by the more or less globular shape of the cast, and the variation should still be well within the tolerances found among ancient coins.

The sprue is cut off and the point of attachment is smoothed over, usually by filing, sanding, and burnishing. Another excellent means of disguising this area is to pack the entire cast, except for the spot to be repaired, in a wad of special insulating putty[8] and then use a needle torch to actually *melt* a small puddle right on the coin's edge. This will blend in and replicate the surface detail of the edge of an ancient coin perfectly.

---

[8] Available from jewelry manufacturing supply sources.

As pretty as his work may look at this point, the forger would be very unwise to consider it finished. Original ancient coins have been kicking around for a long time, and most of them show the effects of their age.

Clean, near-perfect ancients are the exception, rather than the rule, as to what is routinely encountered. One of the main reasons the forger selected the cleanest, finest example of an original he could obtain to use as his master was so that he could "distress" his own creations, giving them each an appearance of authenticity and a semblance of individuality.

"Worn" surfaces should actually be *worn* — not merely the cast detail of a worn surface. Gold and silver ancients are often counterstamped with banker's marks, or even occasionally hacked with a test cut. Bronze coins frequently exhibit surface pitting, and are usually heavily patinated. True, all of these effects have a tendency to lower the visual appeal and value of a coin — but when the "coin" is really just a mass-produced forgery with no actual value at all, anything that contributes to the illusion of its genuineness helps it to avoid detection, and thus creates value for the forger. The application of these effects, *wear, aging, and patina*, are covered in a later chapter.

These four Alexander tetradrachms were hand struck (in October, 2003) from the same set of hand cut dies. Note the slight variation of centering as indicated by the positioning beads at the border. No two hammer-struck ancient coins — even if they originate from the same dies — can ever be exactly identical.

The greatest advantage of the casting process — the predictable, faithful, and repetitive reproduction of the detail found on the master — is also its greatest drawback. Modern machine struck coins, which are *supposed* to all be identical, have standards and a fabric that cannot be successfully duplicated by casting; whereas ancient hammer struck coins, which *do* have properties that lend themselves to casting, are by their very nature unique and individual specimens. No two are ever exactly alike. Even if they are products of the same set of dies, genuine ancient coins *always* vary in size, shape, weight, centering, quality of strike, and overall distinguishing characteristics. It would therefore be quite foolish for a forger to attempt to offer more than a single casting derived from the same master to any one potential buyer.

These four castings were made using one of the previously shown coins as a master. Note that they all share identical features which distinguish them as originating from that same coin. (The casting sprues have not yet been removed from these coins.)

Also, cast forgeries are simply not foolproof. They *can* be detected — even the very, *very* good ones — if sophisticated enough tests are performed on them. The forger's object must be to develop a marketing strategy which increases the odds of successful deception by avoiding such tests, and at the same time fosters a strong assumption of the coin's legitimacy. (This is especially important since ancient coins tend to trade somewhat less commonly than other types of numismatics.) He can do this not only by simulating wear, aging, and patina, but also by making some effort to establish a false or presumed provenance for his wares.

One of the easiest ways of achieving this is to employ counterfeit packaging. There are a number of prominent dealers who specialize almost exclusively in ancients, and who enjoy excellent reputations as a result of their ability to fully guarantee the authenticity of each and every item they represent. Their coins are typically packaged in soft, clear vinyl double-sided envelopes, with one side holding the coin and the other side containing a small printed card with the dealer's name on it. The envelopes, of course, are a standard numismatic item which anyone can purchase at any coin store by the hundred — but the *card* is a feature unique to the dealer, since it bears the well-recognized name and address of his business. It is painfully simple for a forger to reproduce this card on a standard copying machine, thus making his packaged forgery appear to have originated (at one time, at least) from a reputable dealer.[9] This type of "instant provenance", especially for a moderately priced coin, is remarkably persuasive.

While well-made cast forgeries can be convincing, their practicability, as we have seen, is pretty much limited to the thick, irregular properties of ancient coins. Successful forgery of modern coins, on the other hand, can really only be achieved by striking with dies. There *is* a way, however, to combine the best features of *both* methods by taking advantage of the faultless replication of detail possible with casting in order to eventually create high quality steel dies for striking. I'll be getting back to this idea shortly, so in the meantime I ask the reader to remember just three words: *explosive impact copying.*

But let us move on for now.

---

[9] Chances are the forger will have obtained the original coin for his master from just such a source, thus providing himself with a convenient card to copy, as well.

Chapter Five

Methods of Forgery: Creating Dies, Part I

If I could sum up in one phrase all of the lessons learned from more than thirty years experience restoring, conserving, and reproducing antiques, it would be this: The only way to reproduce a thing *exactly* is to produce it *exactly as the original* was produced.

For a coin, this means striking it from a set of dies. Only die striking is capable of duplicating every telltale characteristic, every essence, every subtle nuance of the essential fabric of an original die-struck coin.

But to do this the forger will need to have access to perfect dies — something that was never intended by governments or official minting agencies to be readily obtainable. He will have to make his own. This has always been the most challenging task confronting counterfeiters and forgers, since the dies must be flawless if the coin is to be perfect.

Up until the latter part of the eighteenth century or so, all dies for real coins were usually cut by hand using an assortment of simple tools (and anywhere from a mediocre to a considerable level of skill), resulting in a great many die varieties for any single coin type. Since that time dies have normally been produced by processes involving the use of sophisticated three-dimensional pantographically reducing milling lathes, which are capable of incredible intricacy and complete uniformity. But surprisingly, even lacking such equipment *it is much easier for a forger to duplicate dies for these later coins than for the earlier ones* — which is exactly the *opposite* effect from what the minting authorities had intended!

How is such a thing possible? Well, the truth is that while die making may have always been a technologically progressive field for legitimate coinage, the same has also been the case with numismatic forgery.

There are four practical ways for forgers to create dies: *cutting by hand, plating, casting,* and *hubbing.* The first, because it is the most difficult and affords the least consistency, is really only suitable for producing ancient or medieval types of coins. But the other three, which work marvelously well with modern coinage, have been devised and refined using all sorts of tricks and short cuts until the processes have become appallingly simple and foolproof.

We'll be taking a good, detailed look at these newer developments presently, but first, in order to better appreciate just how and why they came about, it will be helpful to understand how coin dies are made the hard way.

Cutting Dies By Hand — Background

Human nature being what it is, the history of creating false copies of coins is probably only a few weeks younger than the history of coinage itself. And since alternative technology had yet to be explored and developed, the first forgeries (actually counterfeits) were made in precisely the same fashion as the originals — by striking with a hand engraved die.

The designs on these earliest dies were simple, varied considerably, and were often rather crudely done, conditions which offered so few obstacles to those who would copy them that about the only deterrent option available to governments was to impose severe penalties (such as death or dismemberment) for counterfeiting. Eventually the artistic quality of official dies improved, and the challenge of creating convincing false dies increased correspondingly. Governments usually monopolized the talents of the best engravers — partly as a matter of local or national pride, but also largely to produce coins that would be as difficult to copy as possible.

And yet copies abounded, nevertheless. Bronze and other base metal coins were frequently cast using clay molds made from a real coin, while "silver" and "gold" counterfeits were struck on base metal slugs that had been solder plated or fire-gilded.[1] The counterfeit dies used to strike these coins often produced results that looked at least as good as the legitimate coins in circulation, and sometimes even better! (During the declining

---

[1] As the purpose of counterfeiting is to create a profit from nothing, it would have been rather pointless to have struck fake coins from actual precious metal when real coins were worth no more than the metal they were made from. Planchets for "silver" coins were often made by fluxing a slug of heated copper and touching a silver wire to it, thus plating it with a thin layer of silver solder. "Gold" planchets were usually prepared by mixing a pinch of gold dust into a puddle of mercury, rubbing the blank with this mixture, and then heating it to evaporate the mercury. This "fire-gilding" technique leaves behind a strongly bonded, very thin layer of gold on the planchet's surface. Such methods would never be used in modern forgery, of course, since duplication of the correct properties of an original coin is the paramount consideration of a forger, and the intrinsic value of the metal in a forgery is of no importance whatsoever.

portion of the Roman Empire, for instance, some truly abysmal coinage issues were officially produced.) These counterfeits circulated, too. In fact, they became so prevalent within the circles of commerce that it became common practice for bankers (money changers) to make test cuts or place authentication marks on genuine coins which passed through their hands — a situation which may be of historic interest to modern collectors, but which still strikes us today as aesthetically deplorable.

Actual die-struck *forgeries*, though — as opposed to counterfeits — first begin to make their appearance during the fifteenth and sixteenth centuries, when Italian gentlemen of the Renaissance started becoming intrigued by the art and culture of the ancient world. The demand for quality specimens of the masterpieces of classical Roman coinage — particularly the large, bronze Imperial issues — soon outstripped the available supply, and wealthy patrons began to commission medalists to create copies for them to round out their collections. A few artists, such as Giovanni de Cavino of Padua, produced some breathtakingly beautiful replicas during this period. Most of these copies were probably created without the intent to defraud anyone at the time, but it is impossible to say whether this was always the case or not.

During the next three hundred years coin collecting passed from being a mere Renaissance fad into a full-fledged European hobby, and the modern field of numismatics was born. Collectors still remained largely confined to the wealthy leisure class, and their primary interest continued to lay with objects of the ancient and classical world, but this was sufficient. A ready market place, however limited, had developed for a specific product, however specialized. Conditions were just right to favor the rise of the professional numismatic forger.

The great pioneer of this innocent era was an enigmatic German die sinker named Carl Wilhelm Becker, who ranks as possibly the earliest and certainly one of the most prolific numismatic forgers of all time. Active during the decades of the late eighteenth and early nineteenth century, he ultimately produced hundreds of specimens copied from virtually every major ancient series — anything and everything from the commonplace to the ultra-rare. Practical and resourceful as well as creative, Becker also devised ingenious methods for fabricating authentic planchets and processes for "aging" his creations — techniques which are still widely employed by forgers today.

Part of the price of this sort of fame is relegation to folklore, and many myths and stories have grown up around Becker and his works. One of the most persistent (and believed) is that his forgeries were supposed to have been so well done that some are *still* being represented in museums as genuine coins. With all due respect to a unique and fascinating individual, though, this just isn't very likely. There are three very good reasons why.

For one thing, as today's sophisticated collectors (and forgers) should know, practically every ancient coinage issue has been exhaustively cataloged and described during the course of the past century or so.[2] We may encounter an occasional new die variety from time to time as new hoards are discovered, but most types are quite well understood and far easier to authenticate today than they were in Becker's time. Die-struck forgeries of ancients from well cut dies can and still do get past the inspection of many dealers, of course, but the same items are certain to be exposed eventually if they are ever subjected to careful, professional scrutiny.

Second, while Becker's forgeries may have been good, they just weren't *great*. Becker was a talented artist in his own right, and consequently all of his hand engraved dies are a subconscious reflection of *his* talent and skill — not necessarily that of some ancient die cutter. Each period of history produces an artistic "style", an interpretation of form and line that manages to subtly work itself into the artist's way of depicting a subject. Becker was unable to avoid this, and thus all of his "coins" suffer from the contemporary flavor of his own time, a condition which is especially evident in his portraiture. This one factor is the fundamental weakness of practically all hand cut forger's dies.

Lastly, the works of Becker (like all things notorious) have themselves finally achieved status as collectables. As such they are subject to the basic laws of supply and demand, and in some cases the forgeries have become even more valuable than the original coins they were copied from!

As the scope of coin collecting broadened and spread from the mid-nineteenth century on, a variety of struck copies (some legitimate, some not) appeared of American colonial pieces, Spanish pieces of eight, and so forth — most of which were struck from hand cut dies. Some of these which were created as intentional forgeries (rather than as "souvenir

---

[2] This cataloging process has been quite thorough and professional, but it was not without its share of difficulties when it first started out. A few of the earliest type catalogs had illustrations based (quite naturally) on the best examples of coins that they could locate — which often just happened to turn out to be one of Becker's forgeries!

pieces") were actually quite good; most weren't, however, and can be considered the clumsy products of amateurs.

The next truly professional forger of any real consequence was the great Christodulos, who came along about a hundred years after Becker. His hand cut dies were so good (and their products so convincing) that they were finally confiscated by the Greek authorities sometime shortly after 1900 — but not before Christodulos had come out with an astonishing total of nearly 1,000 varieties of ancients! (Fortunately for modern authentication's sake, plaster impressions of all of his dies were made and published for reference.)

If any forgers since have ever been able to come close to such an output using hand cut dies, they have managed to remain unknown.

The emergence of a modern-day Becker or Christodulos is still a very real and sobering possibility, though. Extensive cataloging may have made the eventual detection of forged ancients a probable likelihood, but no such work has yet been completed for the vast and complicated field of medieval coinage — an increasingly popular and highly vulnerable area.

Cutting Dies By Hand — In Practice

Needless to say, a hand cut die would only be used to strike forgeries of coins that were originally struck from hand cut dies. This is because each hand cut die, like the hammer-struck "coins" it will produce, is a unique and highly individual creation. All are made basically the same way, and the quality of each is dependent upon the practiced skill of the engraver. Much of today's "modern" engraving of jewelry, plaques, firearms, and so forth, is accomplished with the aid of specialized power tools, but it would be a big mistake for a forger to attempt to take advantage of such equipment.

To accurately duplicate the effect of a hand cut coin die, the forger must rely upon the old time-honored method of using honed gravers, chasing hammers, burnishers, punches, and patience.

Ideally, a genuine coin should again serve as the basis for the forger's work. But unlike the one used for the casting process described earlier, this coin will not be expected to provide the *specific detail* that would allow the forger to create a copy that is an *exact duplicate* of the original. Such a goal is simply not obtainable when cutting a die by hand. (Even the archaic die cutters, who normally had to make several sets of similar dies for any given style of coin, could never reproduce their own work *exactly*.)

Instead, the genuine coin — along with as many different photographs of similar specimens (usually from books, dealer's catalogs, etc.) as the forger can lay his hands on — will serve as *reference models*. The forger's first task is to try to discern whatever patterns and techniques are held in common by the examples he has assembled in order to allow him to imitate, as closely as he can, the style of the original engravers. The treatment of the pattern of feathers on a bird's wing, for example, or the placement of leaves in a wreath, may be identical from coin to coin — even though there is a slight variation in their individual execution.

Through careful study, eventually the conventions and rules that governed the original die engravers will begin to fall into place and become apparent to the forger, as well. It may seem surprising, but in this way he will actually be able to produce a forgery that is much more likely to be accepted as a legitimate die variation than if he were to attempt to duplicate the specific detail of a specific coin without this "feel" for the original style.

Research and references: Any forger attempting to create hand cut dies will have to become thoroughly familiar with the stylistic characteristics of as many examples of his target as possible in order to imitate them convincingly.

Hand engraving is an acquired skill that requires considerable talent. There is no way that a description of technique, however detailed, can become a vicarious substitute for the practical experience it generally takes years to acquire in order to become a proficient engraver. Moreover, it is beyond the scope or ability of this book to attempt such an effort. At best, I can only hope to give you an idea of a few of the more basic steps and guidelines that a skilled forger would follow while engraving a hand cut die.

Let us assume, then, that the forger has successfully studied his examples and managed to suppress his own stylistic inclinations. The next thing he will want to do is prepare an enlarged linear drawing of each side of the coin, plotting the location and proportion of all major areas of detail. Once again, he will usually work in a scale that will lend itself to easy reduction back to normal size, such as 8:1.

Once the drawings are ready, they are photocopied at full size onto a sheet of clear acetate (of the sort used for making overhead projection slides). This clear copy is then flipped over, placed against a sheet of clean, white paper, and photocopied again. The resulting copy should be a mirror image of the original drawing. This image is then reduced on the photocopier to its normal size, which for an 8:1 enlargement would be 12.5%.[3] Now the normal-sized, mirror image copy is photocopied again onto another sheet of clear acetate. The drawings on this second clear copy will come in handy as templates, which can be repeatedly placed over the work to check it as the engraving progresses.

This linear image will now be transferred to the face of a blank, soft steel die.[4] This may be done by tracing, using the pantograph, making a photographic mask (as was described in Chapter Three under *Alteration by Plating*), or whatever other method the forger, as an engraver, is familiar and comfortable with. The key thing for him to watch for here is to be *sure* that when laying out the image it is *reversed* from the way it should appear on the coin. (I once saw a nicely cut forger's die for a Massachusetts colonial Pine Tree Shilling where the engraver made this mistake. Any coins minted from this die would have been mirror-imaged!)

---

[3] Yes, I realize that there might be a handful of people who are thinking, "But a photocopier won't reduce to 12.5% — most only go to 50%!" This is a good example of why I feel forgers would have to come from the half of the population with an IQ above average. The first copy is reduced to 50%, then *that* copy is reduced 50% to 25%, and then *that* copy is reduced another 50% to 12.5%. *(Sigh.)*

[4] Finished steel dies are always hardened and tempered before they are used, of course. *(See Appendix: Heat Treating of Metals.)*

And then the forger engraves. Again, it would be beyond the scope of this book for me to attempt to explain just *how* he manages to remove exactly the amount of metal necessary to create a perfect, intaglio image of a coin in a slug of solid steel, but trust me here. It can be done. It's kind of like the old line about how to sculpt an elephant — "Take a big block of marble, and chisel away everything that doesn't look like an elephant."

Gravers are basically just tiny little chisels with specially shaped tips, and when tapped with a small hammer they cut away a small piece of metal. When enough metal has been cut away, the new surface is beaten, burnished, pushed, punched, and otherwise coaxed into its desired form. Small pieces of lead are frequently pressed against the engraving as it progresses, inspected, and then the process continues until the whole is completed.

A die being hand engraved — no power tools, no shortcuts, no modern evidence traces.

A hand cut specialized punch, shown next to a coin with matching detail.

Three hand cut dies shown next to coins struck from them. The coins have not yet been aged.

Portrait sketch of Liberty for an early 19th century quarter dollar, and the pantograph master prepared from it.

Left: *A punch blank with the image of Liberty transferred to it using a pantograph. The blank is seven-eights of an inch in diameter.*

Right: *The finished portrait punch of Liberty, which will be driven into a die blank to create the reverse intaglio image used to strike coins. While the pantograph can be of great assistance in laying out an image, the actual engraving of the form must be done by hand.*

Sometimes certain elements of a design were embossed into dies with punches, rather than, or in addition to, being cut. Often these were rather simple — no more than a slightly rounded point, for example, used for applying a beaded boarder, or a short line, or a circle, or whatever. Many of the devices and legends on medieval coinage were applied with nothing *but* a series of small, standardized, wedge-shaped punches, which were combined individually to create the design elements on the coin. As the development of dies progressed, punches became more and more elaborate, incorporating individual letters and numbers, figures, and ultimately even full portraits. The forger will have to make any of these specialized punches he requires, as well.

Forgeries that are hammer-struck from such dies on properly prepared planchets will exhibit every true characteristic of the authentic, individual coins they are based on, and are very hard for anyone but an expert to detect. As you can see, though, the creation of hand cut dies of this level of quality requires not only a substantial investment of time and care, but a level of skill and talent that are frankly beyond the ability of most forgers, potential or already practicing.

The die making methods that follow are not.

But before we go on to them, let's pause here — just for a moment — in order to remind ourselves what a die does, and how it works.

A die, of course, is simply a piece of metal bearing the intaglio image of a coin. When it is pressed with force against another piece of metal, a planchet, the planchet is deformed as its metal conforms to the image in the die, producing a coin. The reason it happens this way is that the planchet is softer — or more *malleable* — than the die is. In order for coinage to work, the die *must be less malleable than the metal being coined.*

Everyone can appreciate that a hardened steel die is less malleable than a copper cent, and anyone who has ever hammered a copper cent into a block of lead (in this case, the coin is acting as a "die") has seen that the coin is less malleable than the lead is. If, somehow, it were possible to make this piece of lead with the image on it less malleable than copper, then it could turn right around and function as a die itself, and be used to mint accurate copies of cents.

But lead cannot be made less malleable, of course. In fact, generally anything that is malleable enough for a coin to be driven into is, by definition, less malleable than the coin, and therefore unsuitable for use as a die. The classic problem that has always confronted the forger is how to take the image directly from a malleable coin and transfer it onto a piece of metal that is less malleable than the coin material, and thus capable of serving as a die.

And that is precisely the problem that each of the following methods, in one way or another, has solved.

Creating Dies By Plating

We have seen how useful the electroplating process can be when working with various forms of forgery by alteration (Chapter Three). But I also promised at one point in that same chapter to eventually show you how perfect dies can be created "for any coin, from any coin". Well, the easiest and surest method of doing so is by using electroplating. In fact, this method is so accurate that each set of dies ends up being an exact, custom, glove-like fit to the specific coin that is used to create them — right down to the tiniest scratch, nick, bruise, and lint mark.

Four metals were mentioned previously as being useful to the forger during electroplating — gold, silver, copper, and nickel. One of them is harder than any of the malleable alloys normally used for almost all modern coinage during the past three hundred years. That metal is nickel. Only coinage of pure nickel, such as that of Canada, cannot be successfully minted by nickel dies.[5] If the forger is able to plate a thick enough shell of nickel onto a coin face, and then *remove* it all in one neat, clean piece, this plated shell can serve very nicely as the working surface for a coin die.

In actual practice, the procedure for accomplishing this is only a little less complicated than it sounds.

Only one side of a coin is prepared to be plated at a time. The opposite side receives a coat of insulating varnish which should extend over the rim of the coin and about halfway across its edge (where the thickness is measured), effectively dividing the coin into two equal halves — one insulated, one bare. The clip from the cathode wire is attached to a bare

---

[5] Remember, the only criteria for die material is that it *"must be less malleable than the metal being coined."* Nobody ever said dies had to be made of steel! Historically, the earliest dies were often bronze, and they held up just fine for the smaller production life that was expected of them.

spot on the coin's *edge* (not the rim), and the coin is ready to plate. Before it is placed in the plating solution, though, the bare surface of the coin is given a light but thorough dusting of fine, powdered graphite (crushed soft pencil lead), applied with a soft watercolor brush.

The first layer of plate the coin receives is copper, which will bond nicely with the graphite to form an initial, ultra-thin shell for all subsequent layers to "grow" upon. Really, it is no more than enough to color the area being plated. Following a gentle dip in distilled water to rinse, the coin can then go into the nickel plating solution and be given a good, strong layer of nickel. But then it is withdrawn, dip rinsed, and returned to the copper solution again for another light, thin layer. The forger continues moving the coin back and forth thus, alternating thin layers of copper with the thicker layers of nickel, until the desired thickness of his "shell" has been achieved — which will be roughly 1/2 to 2/3 the thickness of the coin, or at least 3/32".

After the final layer of plate has been added, the forger detaches the cathode clip wire from the coin's edge (if he can! — otherwise he'll just leave it in place for the time being and cut the wire). The coin and shell are still firmly bonded together at this point, but freezing the coin and then dropping it into boiling water will pop them apart with ease. The forger can then remove the varnish from the coin with solvent and prepare the opposite side for plating. The process is admittedly slow and tediously repetitious, but the results are spectacular.

Each shell will resemble a flat, shallow bowl with a short rim (where the plate extended halfway over the edge of the coin), the entire bottom of which will consist of a flawless intaglio image of the master coin. The back of this shell will still show basically the same general relief of the coin's major types and devices, but they will appear vague and rounded and far less distinct. But even though these shells bear the perfect image of a coin in a reasonably durable metal, they are still not completed dies. With a little modification, they will become die *faces*.

The reverse side of each shell will have to be made completely flat and smooth, with no trace of high or low spots remaining at all. The forger achieves this by simply laying a new sheet of fine emery paper (about #400 grit) face up on a flat sheet of glass, laying the shell (back side down!) on it, and slowly moving the shell in small circles with a light to moderate pressure. In a little while, if the forger made the shell the right thickness, all of the low spots can be thoroughly eliminated without ever breaking through into the image. Next a steel die blank[6] is prepared with a perfectly flat face, slightly larger than the coin, for each of the nickel shells to be mounted to. The forger could use soft solder for this (keeping the heat source directed onto the steel die blank, of course) — or even super-glue, if he wanted. The main things he must be concerned about are fixing the shell to lie perfectly flat against the die blank surface, and preventing too much heat from affecting the properties of the nickel. Thus mounted, whatever force is applied to the opposite end of the die will be transferred evenly through the steel to the entire nickel face at once, and thus to a malleable planchet. The final step is to mount each die in his lathe, where the forger will carefully trim away the thin ridge around the edge of the shell that overlapped the coin, leaving the rim (which is actually a feature of the die face) intact.

These dies, mounted in the proper minting machinery, could now be used just as they are for striking forgeries of coins that were originally broadstruck — or minted without the use of a restraining collar. (Examples of such coins would be all early U.S. coinage minted prior to 1836, Spanish colonial and early Latin American issues, most European coinage prior to 1800, etc.) Forgeries of coins that were originally struck within a collar will, naturally, require the use of a collar in addition to a set of dies. (The manufacture and use of collars — an art in itself — is covered in a later chapter.)

Dies with applied nickel faces will not stand up to prolonged, repeated use, of course. (Even *steel* dies can wear out eventually.) But they will be perfectly adequate for striking a number of convincing specimens on well-annealed planchets — and the softer the metal being coined, the longer the forger may expect them to last. (Dies like these would be ideal, for instance, for striking the forged gold dollars and quarter eagles mentioned back in Chapter One.) Also, while die faces prepared from an original coin that was in mint condition could certainly be employed to produce "uncirculated" forgeries, this needn't always be the case. Dies can just as easily be made from an original coin that is, say, AU-50, EF-40, VF-20 — or any other circulated grade. The forgeries struck from them will then be slightly "aged" in the same way (and for the same reasons) as the cast forgeries covered in Chapter Four.

[6] The final dimensions and shape of a set of dies depend, of course, upon the type of minting equipment the forger uses. A typical die "blank", however, may be visualized as simply a soft steel cylinder around 2" in diameter and about 2" long.

There is another use for dies created by plating besides the striking of entire coins, though, which you have probably already surmised. You may recall that when I discussed *embossing* back in Chapter Three, I asked you to imagine a forger being able to return a coin to the *exact same dies* that it was made in — only this time with a mint mark added to them — and then giving those dies just a light hammer tap. Electroplate dies, in this respect, are unparalleled for use by the forger to create such undetectable alterations. What's more, the force of the blow required to raise the tiny mark is so slight that a collar around the coin's edge isn't even needed.

Left: *A reverse die face for a Washington quarter dollar, created by the plating process, without a mint mark.*
Right: *The same die face, with a mint mark added by using a small punch.*

All the forger has to do is make a punch for a small mint mark, and apply it to the die. This is simply a matter of cutting a reverse mint mark into a small piece of scrap steel (exactly the way it was done with the embossing tool from Chapter Three), hardening it, and then tapping the point of a soft steel nail into the mark. This will emboss a perfect mint mark on the end of the nail, which can then be hardened and used to punch the mark into the die. — Or, if he feels that he lacks the ability to engrave a convincing mint mark (and the mark will be on the opposite side of his alteration from the date), the forger will merely make his reverse die from a different coin which does have one, and "mule" it with his obverse die to raise the mark on the original coin.

Dies made for a specific alteration on a specific coin will probably only be used the one time, and then destroyed. But when a forger can raise a D on an uncirculated 1932 Washington quarter that he paid $30 for and end up with a coin that will bring him $400 - $500, or bring up an S on a

1909 Indian cent that he bought for $8 and will easily sell for $200, or put a D on a 1916 Mercury dime — well, the list is about as endless as the forger's imagination. But while the most profit is obviously to be made by altering uncirculated coins, this does not mean that circulated coins are by any means safe. After all, a smart forger will appreciate the fact that any sudden appearance of too many high valued uncirculated rare coins with mint marks may, before long, attract unwanted attention. And, since the electroplating process can create perfect dies *for any coin from any coin*, there is nothing that prevents a forger from using them to add a mint mark *to any coin in any condition.*

All right, that was one easy method of die making. Here's another.

Creating Dies By Casting

As long as we are clear on the idea that any metal less malleable than the one being coined can serve as a die, the most obvious means of replicating detail with perfect fidelity should occur to us: *casting.* By using the lost wax process to cast the intaglio images of dies, rather than the positive image of a coin, the forger can easily create excellent dies for striking successful forgeries. His only limitations are to cast in a material that will be harder than his planchets, and to control differential shrinkage as much as possible. In practice, neither presents any great problem.

Pure nickel, unfortunately for the forger, does not cast well enough to be used for this, though. Neither does copper (which is too soft anyway); and silver — which is less malleable than gold, and could conceivably be used for successfully striking against soft gold planchets — will simply shrink too much to replicate the precise dimensional standards of modern coinage, regardless of whatever countermeasures are taken. Interestingly, it is *gold*, which just happens to be the softest metal typically used for coinage (and would seem the most unlikely choice for die material), which offers the practical solution!

In the jewelry trade, the fineness of gold is usually measured in *carats* (k), with pure gold being 24k, and all alloys of gold proportionately rated according to their gold content (by weight) with other metals. (In industrial terms, gold fineness is expressed more precisely in parts per thousand, such as .999 fine, .887 fine, etc.) But why alloy gold at all?

Well, besides the obvious benefit of "stretching" it to go further, pure gold is simply too soft to hold up well for the things we like to use gold for. So we alloy it by adding certain amounts of different metals and come up with something that *looks* like gold, and *contains* gold, but is *harder* than pure gold. This is an alloy.[7]

The alloy most typically used for U.S. coinage is 90 parts gold to 10 parts copper, which works out to 21-22k — still quite soft, but it wears a little better than coins made of pure gold would. 18k gold is about the practical upper limit for jewelry, with most rings, watches, bracelets, chains, and such being made from 14k or 12k gold. Some gold alloys may contain copper, nickel, silver, tin, aluminum — or even iron — and in the proper proportions can be used to make a gold alloy that is almost as hard as pure nickel.

There are limitations to this, of course. As gold alloy is made less malleable, it also becomes less *ductile*, and is liable to crack with the application of too much stress. The practical lower limit to a gold alloy suitable for service as a forger's die is about 10k. Still, because of gold's exceptional flow properties, these lower gold alloys cast extremely well. (The casting of the rose with the aphid on it described in Chapter Four was done in 12k gold.)

While the detail and proportions of such casts are excellent, the reader will recall that the greatest problem associated with casting — differential shrinkage — is accentuated if the object being cast is thin and flat. The forger compensated for this by casting only coins that were normally thick and globular. Gold (and gold alloy) castings demonstrate less differential shrinkage than other metals, but the forger can minimize the effect even further by doing the same thing when casting die faces. A die face doesn't *have* to be as thin and flat as the electroplate example we just looked at; as long as the surface bearing the coin's image is flat, the rest of it can be made thick and globular. By thus combining the benefits of alloy and shape, the measurable effects of differential shrinkage on the die face will be minuscule.

Obtaining an incuse image of a coin to make a casting of is actually a matter that has already been brought up — the forger simply planes two

---

[7] The easiest explanation I've heard for what an alloy is and how it works goes something like this: Metals are made up of molecule-sized crystals that are tightly bound together, with open spaces in between them at their corners. When other metals with different-sized molecules are added (suspended in solution), they fill in the spaces, making it more difficult for the original molecules to be moved. The resulting alloy therefore is less malleable — and thus harder — than the original metal.

blocks of pure lead smooth, places a coin between them, and squeezes them together between the jaws of a vise.[8] He then builds a small form around each image — which may consist of nothing more than a short piece of PVC tubing — and pours it full of RTV rubber. This is the lower half of his mold. He can then machine a simple master on his lathe that will be the size and shape of the die face casting, and a similar mold is prepared of it. When the two molds are joined, the finished wax models it produces will resemble the master, only with the incuse image of the coin on their lower faces. They are invested and cast as already described with a centrifuge, and then mounted on steel die blanks. After finish turning the edges on a lathe, the dies are ready for use.

The negative image of a coin made by pressing the coin into soft lead.

An even simpler method, for the forger who is in a hurry, is to simply drip melted investment wax over the positive rubber image of the coin. This will give him a thin wax die face which can be built-up from behind by attaching a thick cone of softer, sticky wax (like beeswax) to form a globular shape suitable for casting. After casting, of course, the back is machined away, leaving a nice, thin die face.

---

[8] Soft, pure lead will not harm the surface of any coin being pressed into it.

An RTV rubber die face mold (positive image of the master coin), with wax die shells made by simply dripping melted investment wax over the face of the mold. When cast, these shells are machined and finished into workable die faces.

Dies made in this manner with gold alloy faces are most suitable for minting forgeries of gold coins, or other coins having fairly soft planchets. They have certain advantages over electroplate dies in that they are less time consuming to make, are more substantial and will normally last longer (for the production of a larger number of strikes), plus any number of dies can be made from a single set of molds — even if the original master coin has been sold or is otherwise no longer available. The crispness of the detail is only slightly less sharp than with electroplate dies, and for all practical purposes is visually unnoticeable — especially on a "circulated" coin. Again, the gold dollar and quarter eagle forgeries mentioned in Chapter One could just as easily have been struck using cast dies.

Assuming the planchets have been prepared of the correct alloy and weight, and the collar is made to the correct size, any coin struck from such dies would have perfectly correct standards. About the only way to possibly detect it as a forgery would be to superimpose a magnified photograph of its surfaces over the image of a known genuine coin, and try to discover any minute differences in the scale of the devices and figures on the coin's face. The risk of this to the forger is less than slight

— I don't know of any coin purchaser who has even heard of such a procedure, let alone would be willing to employ it on every, single coin ever offered them.

That makes two methods of die making that any forger is easily capable of. Here's another.

Creating Dies By Hubbing

The term *hubbing* refers to the process of creating a die by stamping the image of a coin into a die blank with a single, large punch — or *hub* — bearing the surface detail of an entire coin. This is the procedure that is used today to make all production dies for legitimate coinage, and is simply the logical outgrowth of the development and use of more and more complex punches during the evolution of the die making process. These official hubs, of course, are made of hardened steel, in order to be able to press an image into a steel die blank.

With one exception (which we'll get to presently), the forger does not have access to anything that could serve as a steel hub to make an impression with on a steel die. The only thing he does have access to — as always — are the genuine coins he wishes to appropriate the images from. If he is to employ hubbing by pressing a genuine coin into something, then obviously steel is out of the question.

In fact, it doesn't seem apparent that he could make much use of *anything*, does it?

A little while back, I mentioned that "generally, anything that is malleable enough for a coin to be driven into is, by definition, less malleable than the coin, and therefore unsuitable for use as a die." And this statement is true, too, or I wouldn't have made it. But the fact is that it is only *generally* true — or true about 99% of the time. Amazingly, a coin — some coins, anyway — *can* be driven into something that is softer than the coin, which can in turn be used as a successful die! This is due to a phenomenon known as the *brockage principle*.

A *brockage* is a spectacular, highly sought after mint error that is largely made possible by the modern mechanization of the minting process. It occurs when a freshly minted coin, for some reason or other, becomes stuck to one of the dies as it is being made, and another blank planchet is fed into the press without the first coin having ejected. When this second planchet is struck, it receives the impression on one of its sides from a die and on its other side from the stuck coin. The stuck coin, acting in this case as a "die", impresses an intaglio image into its side of the planchet, creating a brockage.[9]

Granted, this is all very interesting — but just *why* this happens is what is of interest to the forger. In order to prolong die life and receive as clear a strike as possible, planchets are always *annealed* prior to striking, in order to make them as soft and malleable as their alloy will allow.

When a planchet is struck between the coinage dies, its metal becomes compressed as it flows into the die images — in essence squeezing its molecules slightly closer together for an effect known as *stress hardening*. The finished coin has just been made slightly harder (less malleable) than the planchet it started out as; this is why it is capable of impressing an image into a second annealed planchet. But the *second* planchet (the brockage) *also* becomes stress hardened in striking, and since it bears an intaglio coin image, it could conceivably function as a die!

Naturally, it would be impractical (as well as stupid!) for a forger to attempt to acquire rare and expensive genuine brockages to use as dies for forgery. Besides, anything a mint can do by accident a forger can usually duplicate on purpose.

By taking advantage of the brockage principle, serviceable die faces can easily be fashioned from well-annealed planchets of proper alloy. The forger merely has to fabricate a simple, three-piece device consisting of an *anvil*, a *collar well*, and a *trussel* in order to do so. (See drawing next page.)

The *anvil* is just what it sounds like — a thick supporting base that the "work" is laid upon in order to have the hammer force applied to it. The only critical dimension is of the small circular pedestal in the center, which must be the same diameter as the coin which is serving as the master. The height of this pedestal is merely enough to support the collar well, which fits over it.

---

[9] Ancient brockages are also known, but there is disagreement among numismatists as to how they could have been produced, since hammer-striking of coins requires considerably more personal attention than mechanized minting. I have such a brockage in my own collection (a Roman dupondious of Trajan, ca. 91 A.D.), and in my opinion it appears too perfectly done to have been the result of a careless accident. My own theory is that they were probably created deliberately by bored mint workers.

The reason I call the second part of this apparatus a *collar well* is twofold: First, it functions as a *collar* to prevent the outward flow of metal as the planchets are struck.[10] Without it, the master coin would also have a tendency to spread ever so slightly as it is further compressed, which the forger will certainly want to avoid.

It should therefore go without saying that the inside diameter of this collar must conform to the exact diameter of the coin. This is a *plain* collar, with the sides finished smooth, since even a coin with a reeded edge will be restrained in a smooth collar while the forger strikes a brockage from it. (The amount of force required simply isn't great enough to cause damage to the detail on the coin's edge.) The second reason is that the piece serves as a *well*, or guide, for the third part to move within.

The last piece, the *trussel*, is simply a plain-faced upper die shaped like a cylinder that sticks up above the collar well high enough to be struck with a hammer. It is machined to fit snugly into the collar well, but slide freely up and down without friction.

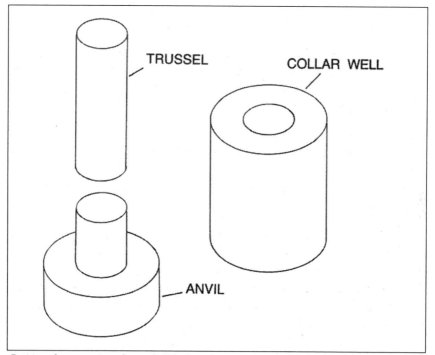

Position of master coin and annealed blanks within the hubbing fixture for creating die shells using the brockage principal.

10 The manufacture of various forms of collars are discussed in detail in Chapter Seven.

The entire assemblage is really nothing but an extremely simple form of a portable, hammer-striking minting machine, with plain, flat die faces. (I'll be showing you a slightly more versatile version of this same type of device a few chapters from now.) To use it the forger sandwiches his master coin between two annealed and polished blank planchets, places them on top of the pedestal on the anvil, slides the collar well over them, lowers the trussel die into place, and gives the end of it a good, sharp rap with a hammer.

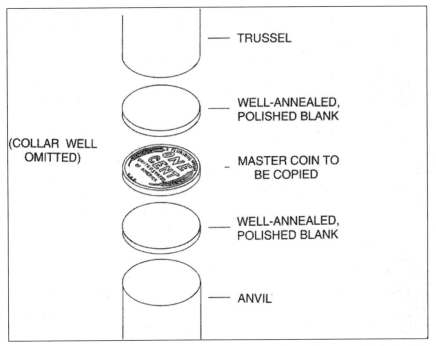

Position of master coin and annealed blanks within the hubbing fixture for creating die shells using the brockage principal.

A funny thing about brockages, though — genuine ones usually aren't as clear and perfect as the ones a forger can produce. Surprised? Here's why:

A full-sized coining press at a legitimate mint is capable of exerting an enormous amount of force — far more than a forger can manage by the single swing of a hammer. Such a machine will easily strike a coin or create a brockage with a single stroke, whereas a forger will need several hammer swings to do so. But this is where he has the advantage. As a brockage is being struck, the annealed planchet begins stress hardening the instant it starts to receive pressure from the coin pressing into it. On a one-stroke minting machine — even though it operates very fast — the annealed planchet still becomes stress hardened before the strike is completed. This means that during the latter part of the striking, a *stress hardened coin* is pressing into an *equally stress hardened planchet* — forcing a little of *both* surfaces to give way to each other. The intaglio image of a genuine brockage will be slightly less crisp than a true die image, and the coin face that created the brockage will be slightly blunted, as well.

The forger avoids this by striking the trussel *only once*, which is just enough to begin to "set" the coin's images into the planchets that are above and below it. He then removes them, anneals the planchets again, cleans them with a pickling solution (always a necessary step after annealing), reassembles the holding device, and strikes them again. He repeats this process three, four, or as many times as it takes, always annealing the planchets between each stroke, until the image detail is perfect.

Then he will give them several good, hard, successive strikes to build up their level of stress hardening — making them into serviceable die faces. (This is very similar to how steel dies are manufactured at legitimate mints. Die blanks are usually annealed several times in between being struck by hubs.)

Heat from soldering would diminish the effect of stress hardening, so the die faces will normally be attached to the die blanks with super glue. The forger must also anneal his planchets between strokes when striking coins from such dies, just as he did when making the die faces.

Brockage die faces will not hold up for very long, but they can nevertheless be used to produce several good, convincing forgeries before they start to wear out. They can be successfully created from coins with copper, silver, or nickel alloys, but the softer gold alloys used for coinage are too ductile to become effectively stress hardened.

Let's return now to an idea that I've teased you with a couple of times — namely, the one exception that allows a forger to use a steel hub to create a steel die, and which will also enable him to produce a bronze 1943 cent "that is actually *made* of bronze". By this point you have most likely realized that the steel cent of 1943 is — in the eyes of a forger, at least — essentially a thin, double-sided steel hub. By merely hardening and tempering a 1943 cent, a forger can easily hub either die faces or complete dies out of steel. These can then be hardened, tempered, and used to strike cents in the appropriate bronze alloy of 1942.

Most forgers wouldn't, however. While it is perfectly possible to create a bronze 1943 cent that could defy detection, it is not very likely it would avoid suspicion. The bronze 1943 cent is simply too rare and famous for a forger to realistically expect any coin purchaser to believe that some anonymous rube could just walk in off from the street, slap one down on his counter, and offer it for sale.

Still, there is a more than even possibility that at least *some* of the known 1943 bronze cents presently accepted as genuine may in fact be forgeries. It doesn't take much thought to realize that a small piece of steel can be hardened and driven into another piece of steel, and the technology to do so has been available since the day the first 1943 steel cents rolled out of the mint to anyone who owned a hammer.

But the ability to hub a 1943 cent has implications that go far beyond the possible but improbable creation of a single, spectacular rarity. The reverse of the 1943 cent is common to all Lincoln/wheat cent varieties minted from 1909 to 1958, and the only modification to the obverse during this entire period was to add the tiny incuse initials of the designer — VDB — under Lincoln's shoulder in 1918.

By carefully shaving and tooling away the "43" from the coin's date prior to hardening and tempering it for use as a hub, a forger can create dies that, without too much difficulty, he can add the remaining two digits of the date to — *any date he chooses* from 1918 to 1958. All he has to do is engrave the numbers together on a piece of steel using a pantograph, make a punch of them (this type of punch is called a *date logotype*), and add them to the die — along with any mint mark, as well. By carefully tooling away the VDB from Lincoln's shoulder in the die (the letters will appear slightly raised above the die image detail), the forger can create any variety from 1909 to 1917.

The implication of this is staggering: By using the commonly available 1943 cent as a hub, any forger who possesses even a modest degree of talent and skill can easily produce steel dies for *virtually any Lincoln/wheat cent variety ever minted*, using only the simplest of methods and equipment!

But even this — the potential to create steel dies that can forge an entire type series — is not the greatest threat that can be posed by hubbing. The next chapter will show you one, last, ultimate form of hubbing that uses a method that can make *any* coin of *any* alloy harder than steel. With it, a forger can make perfect steel dies for any coin, from any coin.

Any coin at all.

Chapter Six

Methods of Forgery: Creating Dies, Part II

Explosive Impact Copying

A little earlier we discussed pressing a coin into lead in order to make an image. I also mentioned that this lead image, of course, could not be hardened. Wouldn't numismatic forgery be a simple matter, though, if there were only some way — through wizardry, science fiction, the power of positive thinking, or whatever — to transform that image-bearing piece of lead into a steel die? Or better yet, to transform a coin into a substance so hard that one could actually hammer its image into steel as though it were lead?

Any forger naive enough to try this, though, will end up with nothing more than an unresponsive piece of steel and a flat, featureless disc of metal vaguely resembling something that a few seconds earlier used to be a coin. He could try hitting it harder, harder, and *harder*, but with no better results. The coin will always flatten out long before the steel has time to even think about taking an image from it.

. . . But if he could only get the coin moving fast enough toward the steel — so fast, in fact, that it just plain wouldn't have *time* to spread out before it penetrates the steel's surface. . .

This is exactly the line of reasoning some unknown forger first began following sometime back around the mid-1960s or so, when it must have suddenly occurred to him that the force of an explosive detonation moves much, much faster than any mechanical means can achieve. The result is known today as *explosive impact copying.*

If the notion of using something as soft as a gold coin to punch an image into solid steel seems a bit far-fetched to you at first, you're not alone. Many people I know are usually skeptical when the idea is first suggested to them, but then, most of them are unacquainted with some of the peculiar effects that can be produced by explosives. Back during my early

Army days I was with the Special Forces, and used to occasionally get to mess around with C-4 (plastic explosive), TNT, det cord, and other neat stuff like that. Every now and then we'd encounter some bizarre and freakish effect after we'd set a charge off — things like pieces of straw or tree bark driven into steel girders, for instance. Probably the strangest thing like this I've seen was on a television program a few years ago that showed an artist using explosives to create "nature art". She would place leaves and ferns on top of a steel plate (*leaves and ferns!*), cover them with another steel plate, place her charges on top, and blast away. The images took into the steel very nicely, and I believe the artwork sold for quite a bit, too.

The first explosive impact dies for forgery were probably produced much the same way, although it most likely required quite a bit of experimentation (and the loss of more than a few coins) before somebody finally got it just right.

The beauty of explosive impact copying is that it can produce an absolutely faithful and durable impression of any coin of any size or composition with equal ease. The downside is that it will destroy the original coin. The "sandwich" method of explosive copying will only imprint one side of a coin really well; the other image will usually be too spread out or deformed to be of use (and likewise, so will the coin). To make a successful set of dies this way requires the use of two master coins — one for the obverse image, and one for the reverse.

A further development of explosive copying was reached when it was discovered that successful results could be achieved with far less explosives (and trouble) by simply "shooting" a coin into a die blank. The explanation behind why this works is identical to the reason why a (*very* illegal) bullet machined from solid brass will penetrate a steel plate or an engine block, while a conventional (and perfectly legal) slug made of lead will possibly dent or crack it, but mushroom out and ricochet before it can penetrate through. The *sectional density* of a metal like brass will allow it to maintain its structural integrity under stress for a longer period of time than that of lead can — just long enough at the velocity of a bullet, in fact, to penetrate rather than collapse upon itself. Given a little less velocity and a thicker piece of steel to shoot at, such a brass bullet will leave a nice, clear impression of its nose where it penetrated only part way into the steel before the force of resistance overcame its velocity.[1]

---

[1] This means "when the bullet stopped".

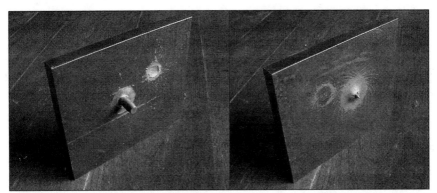

The effect of sectional density: Front and back of a steel plate that has been shot by two rifle bullets — one of lead and one of brass. Though fired at the same velocity, the lead bullet merely dented the steel while the brass bullet has pierced the plate halfway through.

Two downsides to this method: First, a forger needs a pretty big gun to be able to shoot a coin from it. Second, the coin will still be destroyed after imprinting the image from only one of its sides into the die, thus again requiring the destruction of two coins to produce a single set of dies.

Forgers have obviously made this sacrifice before, and will doubtless continue to do so with the more common types of coins they forge — but the fact is that many genuine rare coins are simply too valuable for even a forger to risk exposing them to the explosive impact process. Of course, a forger really doesn't have to, either.

Since a forger is capable of easily producing convincing cast coins and successful cast dies, it shouldn't come as much of a surprise that he can also prepare excellent 14k gold cast hubs to shoot, as well.

The obvious advantages to using cast hubs in this way are that only one original coin is needed to serve as the master, the original coin is not destroyed or damaged in any way, and if the forger miscalculates and his die impressions do not turn out perfect, he can produce as many identical cast hubs from his RTV molds as he needs to until he gets it right.

So far this has been a fairly interesting look at principle and theory, but I'll bet you're ready to turn the page and see just how explosive impact copying is actually done.

Step-by-step, then, here it is:

1. Selection and Modification of Shooting Apparatus

Three considerations are of critical importance to the forger in helping him to decide what he will use to shoot his coins or hubs into his die blanks with.

The first and most obvious is that the caliber (diameter of the bore) of the gun must be slightly greater than the diameter of the largest coin that the forger will create dies for. This actually works out the other way around most of the time, though, with the practical limit of the size of the coins dies can be made for governed by the availability if something to shoot them from.

Second, the barrel must have a *smooth bore* — or an absence of the spiral rifling grooves that normally impart spin to a bullet as it is being fired. A spinning hub would produce a smeared image on a die face, so the forger wants it to exit the barrel nice and straight, with no rotation at all.

And third, the barrel must be long enough to allow all of the propellant in the firing charge to ignite before the projectile emerges from the muzzle, thus assuring that maximum velocity is attained.

If it sounds to you like I'm describing a shotgun, you're absolutely correct. It just so happens that an inexpensive, single-shot 10-gauge shotgun[2] (similar to those manufactured by H & R) makes an ideal shooting apparatus for explosive impact copying.

It will require a minor modification first, though. Shotgun barrels are usually "choked", or slightly constricted at the muzzle in order to hold loose shot patterns more tightly together for longer ranges. Since the forger will be shooting a machined slug containing a hub from the barrel, and not loose shot, the gun will have to have the choke portion of the barrel removed, usually by simply sawing it off. (See drawing opposite page.)

(Not that a forger would probably worry about such things, but it is perfectly legal to cut off the end of a shotgun barrel to remove the choke. The term "sawed-off shotgun", in the *illegal* sense, refers to shotguns that

---

[2] Most American firearms with rifled barrels have their calibers expressed in hundredths of an inch (.22 caliber, .357 magnum, .45 auto, etc.), whereas most shotguns use the term *gauge*, which has its origin back in the old muzzle-loading practice of describing the caliber of a firearm in terms of the number of round balls of bore size that can be cast from a pound of lead. Thus 10 ga. would be larger than 12 ga., and so on. (I know this has nothing to do with coin forgery, but it's interesting to know anyway.)

have been cut to have a barrel less than 18" long. Here's an interesting question, though: Many states impose additional criminal penalties for the use of a firearm during the commission of a crime. I wonder if using a shotgun to create illegal dies in order to commit forgery would qualify? Something to wonder about, I guess.)

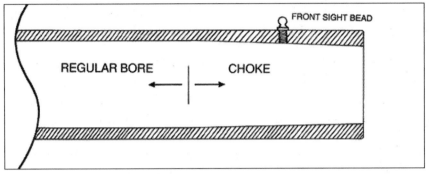

Cross section of a typical shotgun choke.

The reason I've selected a 10-gauge to illustrate this principle is that it is the largest shotgun caliber commonly in use, with a bore diameter slightly greater than three-quarters of an inch. A U.S. cent has a diameter of .750", making it the largest practical coin that can be shot from a 10-gauge shotgun — but of course any coins that are smaller than a cent will also work just as well. For U.S. coinage (both current and obsolete) this would consist of the cent, dime, half dime, silver three cent piece, nickel three cent piece, gold dollar (two sizes), and quarter eagle ($2.50 gold piece). Add to this all 1/10 oz. gold noncirculating legal tender bullion coins (which often have a much higher premium than larger issues), as well as all world coins of similar size made during the last three hundred years, and we have a wide enough field to conceivably provide a forger with an assortment of hundreds of varieties of coins!

Coins larger than the bore of a 10-gauge shotgun will normally be copied using the "sandwich" method, although it is certainly possible for a forger having the right equipment to fabricate a larger shooting apparatus resembling a small cannon. (The construction of such a device would be outside the scope of this book, however. Still, I imagine a forger could probably obtain whatever information he would need for it from one of the book tables at a gun show.)

2. Creating the Projectile Hub

The process used to produce a cast hub is very similar to the one described earlier for making a cast die. A 2-piece RTV mold is again needed — one part containing the master shape of the hub itself (thick and globular), and the other the image of the coin. Unlike the mold used to make the die, however, this second part of the RTV mold will naturally be poured over the actual coin, rather than an incuse impression of a coin.

The metal forms used to make such a mold, and the wax models produced in it, are shown in the illustration and photograph (opposite page).

As you can see from the wax model, the hub looks very much like a small, solid funnel with a complete coin resting against its face. When invested and cast in 10k-14k gold, this will be the image that is fired into the steel die blank. But this cast hub, even with its thick, globular shape, would still make a very poor and unstable projectile if the forger tried to shoot it just as it is.

In order to impart perfect stability to the hub as it is thrust through the length of the barrel by explosive force, it is attached to the front of a machined brass slug about 1" long that has been carefully turned to a diameter .005" less than the shotgun bore. The base (rear end) of this slug should have a slightly concave depression (formed by a countersink bit) in order to take the fullest advantage of the propellant gasses as it is fired, while the nose (front end) is contoured to allow the hub to fit snugly in place, where it is secured with a drop of super-glue.

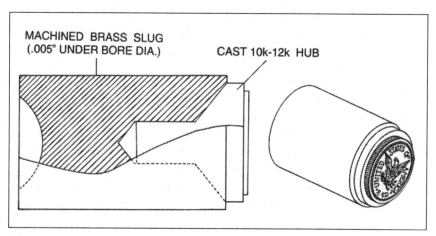

MACHINED BRASS SLUG
(.005" UNDER BORE DIA.)

CAST 10k-12k HUB

The cast projectile hub mounted to a machined brass slug.

Of course, the forger must also use a similar machined brass slug when shooting an actual coin, rather than a cast hub. The only difference would be that the nose is left flat, and the coin simply centered and held in place with super glue. To facilitate the transfer of perfectly consistent force from the slug, through the coin, and to the die blank's surface, the back of the coin (which will be destroyed in the process anyway) must be filed smooth before attaching it to the nose of the slug.

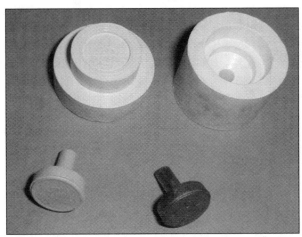

Should the forger find it necessary to reduce the weight of the projectile in order to increase its velocity or propel it with a greater powder charge, the slug can just as easily be machined out of aluminum, rather than brass.

The RTV rubber mold with a wax hub, and a finished casting of a hub in 12k gold.

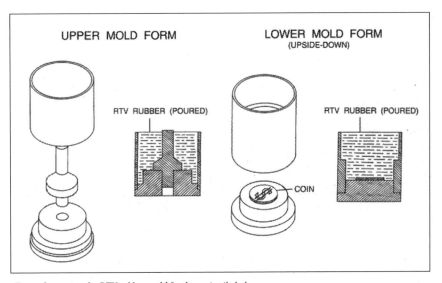

Forms for casting the RTV rubber mold for the projectile hub waxes.

3. Preparing the Cartridge

A highly specialized projectile of this sort requires a highly specialized cartridge case in order to allow it to be properly loaded and fired. An ordinary shotgun shell casing, which is usually made of plastic or cardboard, is simply too flimsy. The forger will have to custom make one — but in order to understand just what he's doing and why, I guess I'd better explain a little bit more about shotguns.

Just as the muzzle end of a shotgun barrel is normally constricted for a short distance by a *choke*, the breech (rear) end of the barrel is enlarged to form a *chamber* into which the shotshell is placed when the gun is loaded. All cartridge-type firearms have such a chamber, which is formed to embrace the shape of the cartridge case.

The chamber in a firearm with a rifled barrel extends just to the full length of the cartridge case, leaving a little shoulder where the front end of the chamber meets the bore. From this point the lands (high parts) of the rifling are beveled slightly, because one of the critical things the cartridge case must do is present the bullet in perfect alignment with the bore — this is why a bullet normally sticks out a little way past the end of the cartridge case. Since the forger is shooting a "bullet" that is a precision-machined brass slug, he will also want his projectile to protrude from his cartridge case slightly into the bore before it can be fired.

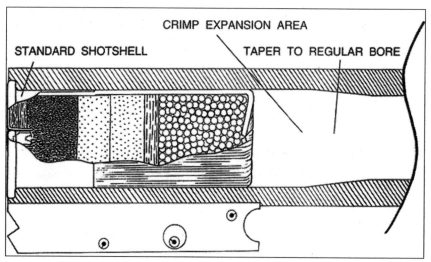

CRIMP EXPANSION AREA

STANDARD SHOTSHELL   TAPER TO REGULAR BORE

A shotgun chamber, shown with the normal shotgun shell it was designed for. Note the crimp expansion area, which tapers to the bore diameter.

But shotgun chambers just aren't made to do this, though. For one thing, the sides of a shotgun shell (being plastic or cardboard) are much thicker than the thin brass tubing of a bullet-type cartridge case — so the shoulder where the front end of the chamber meets the bore is much deeper. The location of the shoulder is also about a half an inch further in than the place where the end of the shell comes to rest, in order to allow space for the "crimp" on the end of the shell (covering the shot) to expand into when the shell is fired.

So even if the inside of a shotgun shell were exactly the same diameter as the bore (which it isn't — not *exactly*, anyway), the shell casing would still be too short to allow the projectile hub to protrude from the end and rest slightly inside the bore. (And believe me, if a flat-nosed brass slug isn't already started into the bore before it is fired, and should catch even slightly on the chamber shoulder, it can cause just all sorts of problems that you really don't want to think about.)

What the forger needs to do, then, is fabricate a special cartridge case that extends to the full length of the chamber, has a well inside its mouth that is the exact diameter of the bore (and is as deep as about half to two-thirds the length of the brass slug), and has very thick walls surrounding a narrow powder chamber. It should also be constructed to withstand repeated use, so I would not be at all surprised if the forger chose to machine it out of steel.

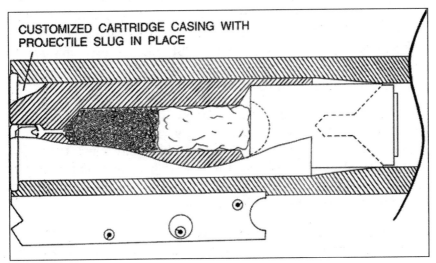

Customized shell casing, with projectile slug in place, in position in shotgun chamber.

A cartridge case of this general sort should answer reasonably well to the forger's requirements. It is also easily reloadable — once the forger has mastered the challenge of determining the proper load for it in the first place.

I have deliberately chosen to say very little about the loading of this 10-gauge projectile hub cartridge. I will make no effort to identify specific brands or charges of powder, for instance, nor will I attempt to speculate about appropriate chamber pressures for any particular brand of shotgun barrel. A forger can find out almost everything he needs to know about these things from any number of reloading manuals, charts, and tables, and can determine the rest through cautious trial and error.

I feel that I ought to at least say this, though. . .

There are three categories of smokeless propellant gunpowder typically used for loading ammunition: pistol powder, shotgun powder, and rifle powder — though there are many varieties of each. The fastest burning powders are used for pistol cartridges, and the slowest for rifle cartridges, with shotgun shells falling somewhere in between, and overlapping in some cases into the pistol powders. *All of these powders have distinct characteristics which suit them to the task they are intended for, and they should never be substituted for each other.*

Loads developed for shotguns, for example, develop chamber pressures of 8,500-13,500 PSI (pounds per square inch), while pistol chamber pressures range from about 15,000-28,000 PSI. The chamber pressures in rifle barrels usually are around 30,000 PSI, but can reach upwards of 52,000 PSI. Obviously, a forger stands a good chance of ruining a tad more than a shotgun unless he is careful.

One rule of thumb that all reloaders go by is that as the *weight of the projectile increases*, there should be a corresponding *decrease in the powder charge* in order to keep pressures within safety limits. The forger will probably begin his trial and error tests with a minimum load that is calculated at being well within the safe range, and will gradually increase his loads until satisfactory results are achieved.

There are just two other things about loading this particular type of highly specialized cartridge that I believe I would speculate upon. One, the empty air space over the powder charge in the cartridge really ought to be filled with loosely packed polyester fiber cotton, in order to hold the powder against the primer and assure even ignition. And two, the brass (or aluminum) slug should be set into the well at the mouth of the cartridge case with a little white glue (like Elmer's) to keep it from slipping out.

4. Construction of Die Blank Holder

Even after all this, the forger would have an easy time of it if all he had to do at this point was set a die blank up against a wall, take aim, and shoot the hub into it. But as you might have expected, it isn't quite that simple. In order to achieve an effective strike, the precise location and angle of the hub's impact must be carefully controlled, and delivered at the point of the projectile's maximum velocity — right outside the muzzle at pointblank range. To attempt to do this freehand would not only be very difficult, but also extremely dangerous. (Worst of all, the forger could risk losing his hub somewhere inside his intestine, and be unable to recover the gold from it for re-use.)

These difficulties are easily overcome, though, by the use of a device which makes explosive impact copying not so much a process as an art form — an incredibly simple die blank holder that slips right onto the end of the shotgun barrel. As the fired hub exits the barrel it enters a small chamber, vents the propelling gasses behind it, slams into the face of the die blank, and drives the entire apparatus off the end of the barrel and into the wild blue yonder — just like one of the old rifle grenade launchers from W.W. II. The slug (with its gold hub) remains trapped in the chamber, and is easily recovered when the die is later detached from the holder.

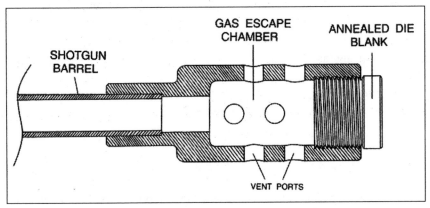

Die blank holder, shown in position on end of shotgun barrel. Note the gas vent holes in the enlarged cavity through which the projectile slug passes.

The main design features of this device are strength, simplicity, and safety. The 1/2" thick walled central chamber is twice the bore diameter and at least twice the overall length of the projectile slug, and is vented by eight 1/2" holes, providing an area 3 1/2 times greater than that of the bore for the gasses to begin to escape through before the hub even reaches the die. (Without the venting of the propellant gasses from the chamber prior to the hub striking the die face, the effect would be the same as the bullet encountering an obstruction in the bore — which would most likely cause the gun to explode.)

The 2 1/2" deep socket in the rear of the die holder is bored to fit without any friction or drag whatsoever over the muzzle of the barrel, which rests against a slight shoulder with an opening that is of greater diameter than the bore, but less than the outside of the barrel. The fit should be so free that if the shotgun were pointed straight down, the die blank holder (which weighs between 4-5 pounds) would fall right off.

Because of this loose fit, it will be necessary for the forger to come up with some method of temporarily keeping the die holder in place until the shotgun is discharged. One simple and effective method would probably be to install a normal shotgun-type bead sight on the barrel about an inch back from the edge of the socket. A thin piece of copper wire can then be looped over this protrusion, and the other end tied to a small stud set into the rim of the die holder socket. When the hub is shot into the die face, this thin wire will easily break. (Or, if he isn't the sort to like to waste a lot of time, I imagine he could simply use a short piece of duct tape.)

The annealed die blank, its surface polished flat and smooth, is secured to the forward end of the heat treated holder by screwing it deeply into a coarsely threaded well, effectively joining the two pieces of steel with a bond as strong as though they were a single piece. The forger will therefore need to prepare each die blank he uses by machining a screw thread onto it. After successful imprinting, the die is simply unscrewed, machined to its final form, and hardened for use.

5. Use of the Explosive Impact Copier

It may sound painfully obvious, but the first step is to load the projectile hub cartridge into the shotgun's chamber, close the action, and engage the safety feature on the firearm. All shotguns have some form of safety. One reason I particularly like the H & R single shot action is because of the simplicity and dependability of its safety features. The gun is not cocked automatically by loading it; it uses an external-type hammer which must be hand cocked just prior to firing. Only when this hammer is pulled back does a cam move up over the rear of the firing pin, allowing the gun to shoot. But whatever type of firearm the forger is using as a shooting apparatus, he will want to be sure that the safety is in good working condition, as he will have to handle the gun somewhat after loading it.

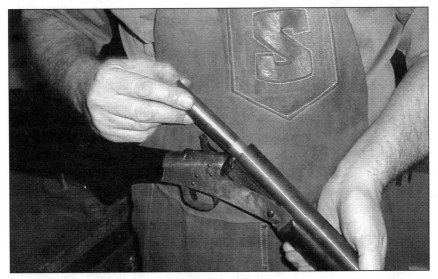

The customized cartridge and projectile being loaded into the shotgun.

Next the forger will take the die blank holder — with a blank die already screwed firmly in place — and slip it on over the gun's muzzle. A short piece of copper wire or tape, as previously mentioned, can be used to prevent the holder from falling off.

Now, with the chamber loaded, the safety engaged, and the die blank and holder secured in place on the end of the barrel, the device should be ready to fire — but here it would probably be wise for the forger to pause a moment, and consider:

The discharging of a firearm, technically speaking, is actually the carefully controlled detonation of a directional bomb. The reason a shooter is usually safe when shooting is that the gun has been carefully

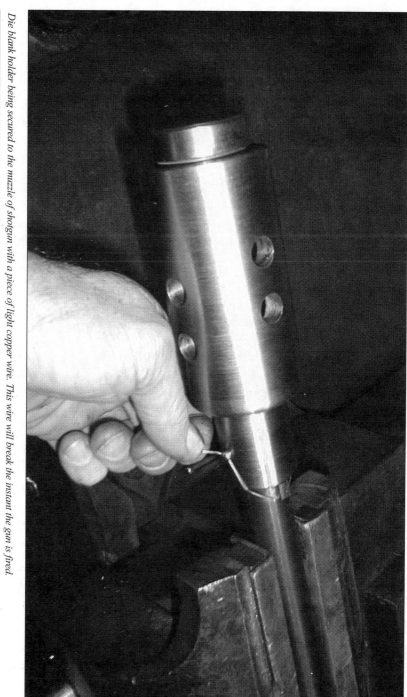

Die blank holder being secured to the muzzle of shotgun with a piece of light copper wire. This wire will break the instant the gun is fired.

A nice, safe shot well, looking down into the collection pit.

Shotgun firmly mounted to ceiling joist, with string for remote firing. Once in place, the gun is cocked and is ready to fire.

BANG!!! *The explosive impact copier doing what it does to earn its name.*

designed, tested, and even over-engineered to safely perform a specifically defined task — i.e., propel a certain sized bullet with a certain amount of force from a certain type of barrel at a certain speed. When a shooter begins to modify this task by — say, changing the type of bullet or the amount of force used to propel it, he is altering a formula that could drastically affect the result of this detonation.

Having never personally witnessed a forger committing an illegal act, I can only speculate about how anyone would attempt to shoot such a radically modified firearm as a 10-gauge explosive impact copier, but there are two schools of thought that would seem to apply. There is the stupid way, and there is the safe way. For the one, the forger would simply pick up the gun, put it up to his shoulder like Rambo with an attitude, aim it out an open window, and squeeze it off in the direction of a nearby brick wall. For the other, he would mount the entire device in a sturdy brace and fire it by remote. (Speaking for myself, I wouldn't want to be anywhere near the thing when it goes off.)

A good, sensible way to use the explosive impact copier would be to fasten it securely to a wall or a ceiling beam pointing straight down, and to pull the trigger using a string from a nice, safe distance away — preferably another room. I think it would also be advisable to shoot into some sort of an enclosed collection pit, like a bricked-in chamber or a steel drum, with a couple of feet of loose sand at the bottom to catch the die holder without damaging it.

The holder requires some torque to remove it from the die blank after shooting.

Once recovered, the rim of the die can be gripped in a bench vise and the die holder twisted off. When everything goes well, a perfect image from the face of the gold hub will be neatly impressed into the solid steel face of the die. This image can then be centered in the forger's lathe and the blank machined to its final configuration before being hardened for use. The machined slug left over from the shooting is not reusable, of course, but the recovered gold from the hub may be used over and over to cast other hubs.

A perfect shot. This blank can now be machined into a finished die form and hardened.

Explosive impact copying using cast hubs rather than original coins is not limited in size to those which can be conveniently shot from a gun, however. Cast hubs for larger coins of virtually any size can also be prepared in exactly the same fashion as for smaller coins, and explosively copied using the "sandwich" method. As long as the configuration of the casting is thick and globular, rather than thin and flat, differential shrinkage with gold alloy will be too slight to matter. After casting such a hub, the forger will simply machine off the rear portion, leaving a thin, flat, one-sided hub suitable for sandwiching.

While explosive impact copying can be a bit time consuming to get set up for, and the forger will need an adequate lathe and some good machining skills, the results certainly seem to justify the trouble. The images obtainable through explosive impact copying are as flawless as the coins they come from, and when used properly, can produce forgeries that are virtually undetectable.

But so, of course, can the other die making methods we've covered. What makes explosive impact copying so unique is that the dies it creates are *steel*. Dies made by plating, casting, or the hubbing of brockages all suffer from being somewhat fragile, and are of only limited use before they begin to deteriorate. Hardened steel dies, on the other hand, are far superior to any other type, and will last for a very long time — long enough to do as many strikes of any one coin in particular that a forger would ever care to do.

And each and every one, from the first to the last, can be absolutely perfect.

Chapter Seven

Collars and Edge Marking

There's an old expression that says something about there being "two sides to every coin" — but every forger knows that isn't really true, and so should you. The most perfect die faces possible will not produce a believable forgery if the coin's edge is wrong.

The edges of coins range from the bulbously rounded cast contours of ancients and the thin scissor formed flans of medieval coins, on through elaborately embossed ornamented patterns and various styles of lettering (both relief and incuse), and finally to the functionally utilitarian sameness of today's collar-formed plain and reeded edges. A coin's edge is an essential and noticeable part of the entire coin's *fabric* — the sensory qualities of a coin that combine to make it "seem" correct.

Whichever type of coin he is working with, an effective forger must be thoroughly familiar with and capable of duplicating the precise effects of the edge. With ancient and medieval coins this doesn't really present much of a problem, since their edges are formed and finished during the creation of the planchets. We'll leave discussion of these hammer-struck coin edges to the next chapter, then, and focus here on the sort of mechanical edges that are deliberately imparted to machine-struck coinage of the last three or four hundred years.

The practice of placing markings and ornamentation on the edges of coins developed in direct response to the widespread threat of *clipping*. One of the simplest ways for larcenous-minded people to make a profit from nothing was to form a habit of trimming small amounts of precious metal from the edges of gold and silver coins as they would pass through their hands. Thin, hammer-struck coins with their plain and often irregular edges were particularly vulnerable to this, and if a person were in a position to handle enough coins — say, as a merchant or a moneylender — he could reap a substantial profit with little risk of discovery. It was therefore reasoned (quite rightly so) that if the edges of coins bore a discernable pattern, clipping could be immediately detected, if not eliminated altogether.

The first efforts at edge decoration were made in the late 16th century by striking the coin within an engraved segmented collar, which acted as a "third die" to impart relief detail. This had the desired protective effect, and the use of collars also produced uniform, perfectly round coins for the first time in history. But the segmented collar, which needed to be separated to release each coin after striking, slowed down minting production.

A faster method was soon developed which involved rolling a design onto the edge of a planchet prior to striking it with dies, but this meant that even a one-piece, plain collar could not be used during striking to assure size uniformity, since it would damage the detail. Striking the coins without a collar, on the other hand, allowed the edges of planchets to spread slightly outward, and the size of finished coins always varied somewhat with the differing amounts of pressure applied during each strike. But uniformity was willingly sacrificed for decoration, and throughout most of the 17th and 18th centuries coins with ornate, relief edges were *broadstruck* without collars.

Only during the early 19th century, when banks finally put pressure on governments to produce easily stackable coins, did the use of collars return to become standard minting procedure, with modern, completely uniform coins the result.

Not too surprisingly, perhaps, it is the edge effect of modern, completely uniform coins that is easiest for the forger to duplicate.

Collars

Modern coinage, as mentioned, is universally struck within an enclosed collar in order to arrest the outward flow of metal from the edge of the planchet, guaranteeing a coin that is perfectly round and of uniform diameter.[1] To understand how a collar works, picture a thick steel disk with a hole in its center — just like a large washer. The center hole is the exact diameter that the finished coin will be. This washer is placed over the lower die, which is machined with a sharply defined neck that allows the die face to enter the collar. A planchet of slightly smaller diameter than the finished coin (more about this in the next chapter) is placed

---

[1] Oh, all right. . . A few world coins are struck within *shaped* collars, so obviously they don't turn out "round". (But they are uniform, which is the whole point.)

inside the collar on top of the lower die, and then struck with an upper die that is also machined with a neck to fit into the collar's hole. The planchet, which is completely surrounded by upper die, lower die, and collar, is thus squeezed into the perfect shape of a coin. The planchet, which is completely surrounded by upper die, lower die, and collar, is thus squeezed into the perfect shape of a coin.

Simple as it sounds, it took coinmakers 2,000 years to come up with the collar.

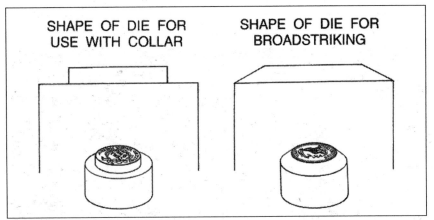

SHAPE OF DIE FOR USE WITH COLLAR

SHAPE OF DIE FOR BROADSTRIKING

Cross section of a die shaped for use with a collar, compared to a die used without a collar (broadstruck coinage).

There are three forms of collars — *plain*, *reeded*, and *segmented*, and the effects of each are well within the scope and abilities of the modern numismatic forger.

1. Plain Collar

The simplest collar of all, a plain collar is merely the washer-like steel disk with a hole in it just described. It is used to produce coins with a plain, perfectly round, unornamented edge such as can be found on the cent, the nickel, and so forth. Plain collars have also been used to strike coins where lettering or designs have been previously applied to the planchets in an *incuse* fashion, such as with older silver coins from Germany. The uncomplicated ease with which they can be made and used present very little challenge to a forger possessing even the most basic tools and equipment.

A plain collar (or any collar, for that matter) doesn't really have to be washer shaped, it can vary somewhat in dimension, finish, or configuration depending on the type of minting apparatus it will fit into.

The only critical area is the hole inside which the coin is struck. It *absolutely must* be the exact diameter of the finished coin, and it must also be polished perfectly smooth. The forger achieves this by first boring the hole a couple of hundredths of an inch undersize, hardening the collar, and then finish grinding the inside of the hole on the lathe using a small grinding tool. About the only other thing he needs to know is that the collar should be about twice the thickness of the coin, in order to allow enough room for the die faces to enter to strike the planchet.

A freshly minted buffalo nickel, still wedged solidly within a homemade plain collar.

When a coin is struck in a plain or reeded collar, it fills the space within the collar so completely that it becomes firmly wedged inside. Ejecting the coin from the collar is simply a matter of pushing it straight out, either with some sort of automatic cam which will slightly raise the lower die, or by removing the collar and pushing the coin out manually.

2. Reeded Collar

The reeded edge found on most coins is formed by the edge of a planchet being squeezed up against and forced into vertical grooves lining the inside of the hole of a reeded collar. While a reeded collar operates exactly the same as a plain collar, it is just a little bit more complicated to prepare.

In order to understand how a reeded collar is made, it will be helpful to think of a coin with a reeded edge as having two diameters, just like a toothed gear wheel. There is an *inside* (minimum) diameter, which is measured at the depth of the grooves around the edge of the coin, and there is an *outside* (maximum) diameter, which is measured at the height of the ridges. These two measurements comprise a critical part of the standards of any particular reeded coin type, so the forger will first take exceptional care to record them accurately from an original coin. It will be necessary to use each in the manufacture of the collar.

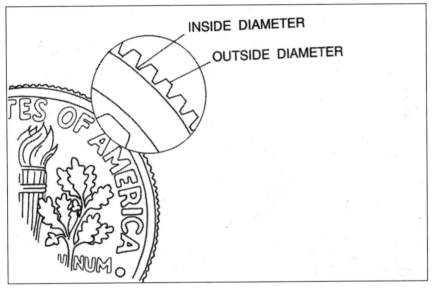

The reeded edge of a coin actually resembles a toothed gear wheel, with an inside diameter and an outside diameter. A forger will find it necessary to carefully measure and duplicate each.

To begin with, the hole of the unhardened steel collar form is machined and ground to the exact inside diameter, and then temporarily set aside. It will be hardened for use only after the vertical grooves are added to it, but this is the part that starts to get complicated.

For one thing, different reeded coin types often have different numbers of "teeth", even though their size may be similar. A Canadian quarter dollar has finer reeding, and therefore more teeth, than a U.S. quarter, for instance. And just as this slight difference in the edge of a Canadian quarter will cause it to visually stand out in the center of a roll of U.S. quarters, so will a forgery with even slightly improper reeding be easily distinguishable from genuine coins. Obviously, then, it is crucial for a forger to determine the precise number of teeth (or grooves, depending on which way you want to look at it) on any given coin before attempting to create a collar in order to forge it.

We'll use the U.S. dime, which has 118 teeth, as an example. The forger will have to cut 118 vertical grooves into his collar, spaced an equal distance apart, to a depth of exactly one-half the difference between the inside and outside diameters of the finished coin. Simple, right?

Well, actually it is. . . sort of. The grooves are all cut together at one time by a process known as *broaching*. Here's how it works:

A cylindrical steel "press plug" about an inch long is turned on a lathe to the exact *outside* coin diameter, and then scored lengthwise all around its circumference 118 times with the point of a sharp cutting tool that has been specially ground to the proper size and shape for the purpose. (This can easily be done on a lathe simply by moving the tool parallel to the stationary work, and rotating the work slightly between each cut.) One end of the plug is then turned to match the *inside* diameter for about a quarter of an inch, with a 2° angled shoulder joining it to the rest of the plug. Then, with a very sharp, 60° pointed cutting tool, four or five fine parallel grooves are cut into this sloped shoulder and the first little bit of the cylinder, creating a progression of tiny cutting teeth.

Using a lathe to cut the grooves onto a reeded broach. The cutting tool must be precision ground to the exact size and shape of the desired "notch" in a reeded coin's edge.

The indexing wheel (made of acrylic) is made to fit onto the lathe's spindle and is held in place by the chuck (which holds the work), so that it and the chuck will turn together. The spring-operated cam lock is used to manually engage the measured notches on the indexing wheel.

When hardened, this plug will be a broach, which is pushed (using plenty of cutting fluid as a lubricant) through the collar form,[2] effectively producing a fully reeded collar.

The trickiest part of making the broach is indexing the work so that the correct number of grooves can be cut. Like the number of teeth on most reeded coins, 118 is an oddball number that isn't rationally divisible by anything. So, in order to divide a 360° circle into 118 equal parts, the forger will find it helpful to make an index plate — which is simply a larger disk that is notched around its edge with the appropriate number of divisions.

Let's say that the forger wanted to make his notches in this plate 1/8" apart, which is a large enough space to be convenient to work with. 1/8" x 118 equals 14.75" — this will be the circumference of the disk he will turn on his lathe. He could divide the circumference by pi in order to determine the diameter, but it is much easier to simply use the 10' diameter tape mentioned in Chapter Two. By making a loop of the desired circumference (lining up 0" with 14 3/4"), the reverse side of the tape will indicate the precise diameter of the loop to within a hundredth of an inch. In this case, it is 4.70". He turns the disk to the proper diameter, marks off 118 points around the edge an eighth of an inch apart, and then notches

---

[2] As a machining process, broaching normally requires a considerable amount of force. In this case, however, such a slight amount of metal is being cut away that only a moderate amount of effort, like the pressure that can be applied from the tailstock screw of a lathe, is necessary to broach a reeded collar.

each point with a triangular file. By fixing this index plate to rotate with the work, and setting up a small pin to lock into each notch as it advances, the forger will have no trouble making whatever odd number of cuts he needs in order to duplicate the reeded edge of any coin.

The setup of the lathe for cutting a reeded broach.

3. Segmented Collar

Easily the most challenging type of collar to make, the segmented collar is also the most challenging type to use. It consists of at least three or more main pieces, each containing an engraved, crescent-shaped portion of the hole in which the coin will be struck. These pieces must be joined and locked together during minting, and then separated following each strike in order to release the coin. Cumbersome, troublesome, and decidedly slow, they have nevertheless imparted spectacular relief designs to the edges of some of the world's most beautiful and famous coins, among them the bold lettering on the silver English crown, and the elegant stars of the Saint-Gaudens $20 gold piece.

Though still in occasional use by some mints for commemoratives or special issues, segmented collars have fallen from favor for normal minting purposes largely because of the slowing effect they have upon production. Also, compared to simple one piece collars, most official segmented collars are complicated devices that have to operate automatically using a great many cams, shunts, and mechanical contrivances in order to function at any sort of production capacity at all.

Speed and mass production capability are matters that are of no consequence to a forger, though. He is after *effect*, and has the luxury of taking his time and ignoring such complications in favor of much greater simplicity, provided he can achieve this identical effect.

One of the easiest ways to accomplish this is to employ a "collar within a collar", which works something like this:

After determining the correct number and size of the collar segments by carefully examining an original coin (a faint seam from the joints is usually evident, particularly on coins that have seen little circulation), the forger will construct a small steel "pie" about one inch greater in diameter than the coin, with each of the wedge-shaped pieces fitting tightly together along their seams. From the exact center, where all of the pieces meet, he will then lay out a circle approximately 1/2" greater in diameter than the coin, or along a point that lies halfway between the outside edge of the "pie" and the inside edge of where the hole that the coin will be struck in will eventually be.

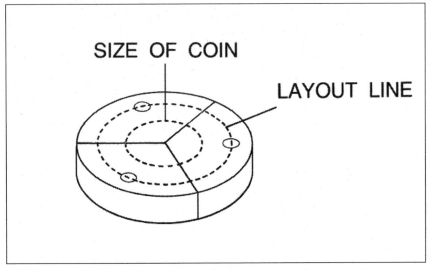

"Pie" segments joined into a disc, showing layout line for screw holes and an outline of the size of coin.

All this circle is for is to provide the forger with a line upon which he can mark and drill one or two small holes in each of the pie pieces, through which he will use screws to fasten the entire thing to a flat-faced mandrel (see description of a mandrel in Chapter Three). He then places this mandrel in his lathe, centers it upon the junction of the pieces, and machines a smooth finish around the outside of the "pie" (which may as well now start to be called the "inner collar").

The forger removes the mandrel from the lathe, measures the new diameter of the collar, and then machines a *second* collar that is simply a plain, one piece ring about a half an inch wide that will fit freely yet snugly around the inner collar. Both the inner and the outer collar are the same thickness.

When assembled, the inner collar pieces could slip and become misaligned within the outer collar, so the forger must devise a means to lock the two collars securely together. A simple way of doing this is to "sandwich" them between two thin, washer-like plates that overlap both the segmented pieces and the locking ring.

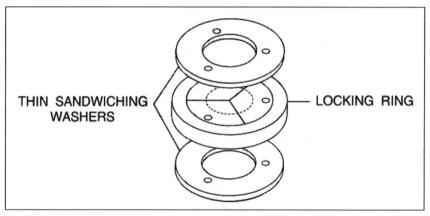

THIN SANDWICHING WASHERS — LOCKING RING

The locking ring is the same thickness as the pie segments.

The small bolt holes in the segmented collar pieces are transferred to these sandwiching washers, and the entire assemblage is then again attached to the mandrel, mounted in the lathe, and centered. The center hole for the segmented collar can now be bored and finish ground to the exact size of the coin. (Note: the center holes of the two thin sandwiching washers are of somewhat greater diameter than the coin well, so that they will not interfere with the entry of the die faces into the collar.)

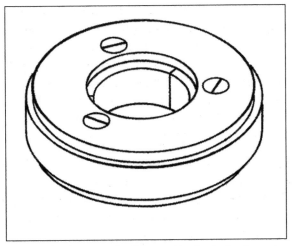

The completed segmented collar assembly after boring the center hole to the diameter of the coin. The individual segments will still need to be engraved.

There wouldn't be much point in going to all the trouble of making a segmented collar if it were just left plain, of course. The detail and designs on the crescent-shaped portions of the coin well will have to be carefully engraved, punched, and otherwise tooled — just as they would for a hand cut die. The reader should by this time realize that, while difficult to do and requiring a fair amount of skill, such hand engraving is certainly not beyond the ability of a talented numismatic forger.

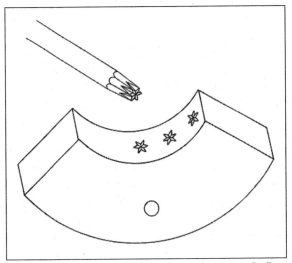

A star punch being used to decorate a portion of a segmented collar.

The segmented pieces are then hardened for use, and the forger has effectively manufactured a simple, segmented collar. To use it he will place short pins, bolts, or screws through the small holes in the sandwiching washers and the inner collar segments, lining everything up and bonding it together. A planchet can then be struck within it just as it would be with any other type of collar. To release the coin, the collar is simply disassembled manually.

One other point should probably be mentioned regarding use of a segmented collar. With almost all collars used to impart relief detail to the edge of a coin during die striking — and particularly those with lettering — there is a "right side-up" and an "upside-down" in relation to the coin's faces. This is because the segmented collars used for legitimate coinage are an integral part of the minting apparatus, and are always fixed to the same orientation with the dies. This means that they cannot be flipped over and used right side-up for some strikes, and upside-down for others.

A careful forger will pay attention to this and always orient his segmented collars the same as on the original coins he is copying.

Edge Marking

At about the time coinmakers were first deciding that segmented collars slowed down their work too much, they really only had three other options open to them.

They could just forget about edge marking and put up with clipping (which was unacceptable); they could switch to one piece plain or reeded collars (which weren't considered "complicated" enough — the feeling was that more ornate designs gave better protection); or they could come up with a whole new, faster way to create relief detail on a coin's edge.

Most opted for the latter, of course, when around 1660 some bright person invented a machine to mark the edges of planchets in a separate step prior to striking them. Within a few years an improved version had been developed that could mark 20,000 planchets in a single day, which pretty much took care of worries about production. Of course, if a large mint needed to handle more than this, they could always just build another machine. They were simple enough to make.

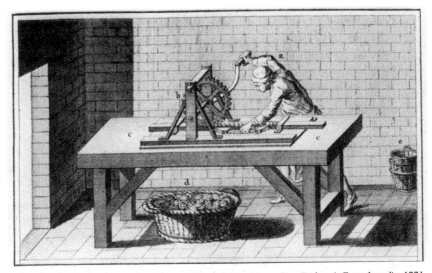

A contemporary illustration of an edge-marking machine in use, from Diderot's Encyclopedie, 1771.

All an edge marking machine consisted of was a horizontal surface containing two flat, bar-like clamps which lay parallel to each other. One of these clamps was stationary, and the other was attached to a gear rack which allowed it to move back and forth, driven by a small gear wheel connected to a handle which was turned by hand. In operation, each clamp held a strip of steel engraved along its edge with the design or pattern to be embossed into the edges of the planchets. The strips were arranged parallel to each other at a distance of about 1/32" less than the diameter of the raw planchets. When the forward edge of the movable strip was aligned across from the rear edge of the fixed one, a blank planchet was placed in between the two and the handle was turned, rolling the planchet along between the two strips and compressing its edge into the engraving. Other planchets could be fed one right after the other behind the first, with as many as ten at a time being rolled along with each operation on the larger machines. Planchets were usually marked prior to being struck as coins, but it was also perfectly possible to mark coins after they had been struck, and both methods are known to have been used. In a busy mint, two or three men on a single machine could potentially mark a hundred thousand coins a week, or over five million a year.

Obviously even the most ambitious forger doesn't need to mark 20,000 coins a day, or even ten all at once. He can construct a much smaller, simpler machine that does exactly the same thing, one planchet at a time.

A homemade edge-marking machine, capable of rolling one coin at a time. It is able to adjust to planchets of various diameters, and its die strips are removable and interchangeable. Any forger with the inclination could design and build such a specialized machine.

With a homemade device similar to the one illustrated here, the only thing that limits a forger being able to replicate any edge marking on typical 18th century broadstruck coinage[3] is his skill as an engraver. Just as with the sections of a segmented collar, this engraving, punching, and tooling has to be done by hand. (This is why it is much easier for a forger to duplicate the edge effects of modern coins struck in one piece collars.)

Still, it certainly can be and definitely has been done. On the positive side (from the forger's view, that is), the devices found on the edges of coins are far less detailed and complicated than those on a coin's faces, and are usually quite simple in their execution. Conversely, since the original design work was done by hand, the forger must still attempt to match the style, skill, and whims of the original die cutter.

The vast majority of edge-marked coins have relief detail that falls into any one (or a combination) of three basic categories:

1) *Patterns* - this may include vines, leaves, twisted cords, etc. Often used on fairly thick coins of larger diameter. (Example: piece of eight, Austrian thaler.)

---

[3] Vulnerable issues of this type would of course include Spanish colonials (escudos, doubloons, pieces of eight, etc.), British guineas and crowns, and early U.S. silver and gold issues, as well as a host of European ducats, thalers, guilders, reales, ecus, louis d'ors, riksdalers, rubles, and so forth, and so on.

2) *Lettering* - may also include figures, such as stars. Most often these were punch applied to the die strip. Usually reserved for thickest coins. (Example: English crown.)

3) *Graining* - close, parallel grooves that have the same appearance as reeding, though applied by an edge marking machine and not by a collar. May be vertical or set at an angle (slanted). Used for thinnest coins, where other types of edge marking would not be practical. (Example: English guinea, early U.S. quarter dollar.)

When the use of collars finally resumed and became widespread around the early 19th century, the use of edge marking machinery did not disappear altogether, however. People soon discovered that designs could also be imparted to planchets in an *incuse* manner, and that striking such a planchet in a plain collar would then have little damaging effect upon the edge detail. This process was most often used with lettered edge effects, and is still widely used today.

Incuse inscriptions applied by edge marking machinery present a bit more of a challenge to forgers than relief detail, though. This is because the steel "die" strips must be prepared with their detail in *relief*, which is usually much more difficult than simply cutting or punching detail into a flat surface in an incuse manner.

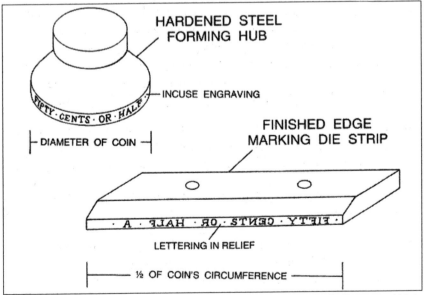

HARDENED STEEL
FORMING HUB

INCUSE ENGRAVING

FINISHED EDGE
MARKING DIE STRIP

|- DIAMETER OF COIN -|

LETTERING IN RELIEF

½ OF COIN'S CIRCUMFERENCE

A hub with incuse lettering, which produces an edge-marking die strip with relief lettering, which is in turn used for marking planchets with incuse lettering.

The most practical way for the forger to create a die strip with relief detail is to use the same method that mints used to use. He will first prepare a steel "edge hub" with all of the coin's edge detail engraved, punched, or otherwise tooled into it. When hardened, this hub is then run through the edge marking machine against a pair of plain, well annealed blank die strips with a single, smooth motion. The die strips are then inspected, finished, and hardened for use. An examination of actual coins seems to show that most often these strips were made to impress detail along half the circumference of a planchet, the other half being applied simultaneously by the other strip.

In order to be sure that the edge hub kept moving evenly and didn't slip while imprinting the die strips, blank areas between words were often originally designed to contain small figures like stars or leaves. When such detail was not desired on the finished coins, sometimes the hub would simply be punched or scored in these plain areas in order to "bite" the die strip better, and the extra unwanted relief impressions that resulted were then polished off from the strips during finishing. This wasn't always done, however.

The edges of a few very early U.S. coins — such as 1809 half dollars — often show these "extra" marks. Similarly, it was sometimes found that a die strip lacked enough relief detail to keep planchets rolling smoothly, in which case it would be given a few incuse punches to help things along. This produced a few small relief areas on the edge of the planchet which would be flattened somewhat by striking in the collar, but still leave some evidence that they were present. (Good examples of this are U.S. half dollars from 1830-31, and the 1811 French Imperial 5 franc piece.) A better forger will look for just such ordinarily overlooked detail to copy.

Since all edge marking, whether relief or incuse, was applied to planchets in a separate step prior to actual minting, the planchets were apt to be fed into the minting machine with either side facing up. In other words, there is no "right side-up" or "upside-down" relationship between the edge of an edge marked coin and its faces — another point that the careful forger will be certain to make note of.

This concludes the portion of this book dealing with the artistic potentialities and limitations of numismatic forgery. By now every collector, dealer, investor, and armchair numismatist reading this should recognize the full implication of what has been brought out in the past three chapters — namely, forgers can pretty much duplicate the precise detail and effects of the front, back, and edge of any coin they want to. The only thing left for them to make a mistake with is the planchets.

Chapter Eight

Planchets

When being examined for authenticity, whether by a purchaser or an authentication service, the first major hurdle that any coin must clear is an evaluation of its *standards*. Tests are made to see if its size, weight, alloy, and types are comparable to those of a known genuine example.

But if standards can be measured by a tester, they can also be measured or learned by a forger. His task is to discover those standards and create a product that will match them. He will manufacture high quality dies to replicate the coin's *types*, and he will control its *size* (with modern coins, at least) through the use of a properly made collar. The remaining two standards criteria, *weight* and *alloy*, will be met automatically if he can simply come up with a proper planchet.

I used the term "come up with" for a reason. The forger can, of course, make perfectly convincing planchets on his own — and we'll be taking a look at a number of ways he can do this — but there is often a much simpler way they can be had. In many cases he merely has to buy them.

Purchasing Planchets

Despite inspection procedures and other safeguards, genuine blank planchets occasionally slip through the coining process and escape from legitimate mints. Once discovered, these blank coins are considered "errors" and are readily obtainable from almost any coin dealer, sometimes at ridiculously low cost. The following examples show suggested retail prices as of this writing (based on 2004 prices) for commonly available blank planchets of U.S. coin types:

- ◆ Large Cent - (pure copper) $76.<u>00</u>
- ◆ Indian Cent - (95% copper, 2 1/2% tin, 2 1/2% zinc)[1] $3.<u>00</u>
- ◆ Lincoln Cent - (95% copper, 5% zinc) $3.<u>00</u>
- ◆ Steel Cent - (zinc plated steel) $19.<u>00</u>
- ◆ Lincoln Cent zinc - (copper plated zinc) $1.<u>50</u>
- ◆ Copper/nickel 5¢ - (75% copper, 25% nickel) $5.<u>00</u>
- ◆ Wartime 5¢ - (56% copper, 35% silver, 9% manganese) $340.<u>00</u>
- ◆ Silver 10¢ - (90% silver, 10 % copper) $10.<u>00</u>
- ◆ Silver 25¢ - (90% silver, 10 % copper) $42.<u>00</u>
- ◆ Silver 50¢ - (90% silver, 10 % copper) $18.<u>00</u>
- ◆ Silver $1 - (90% silver, 10 % copper) $450.<u>00</u>
- ◆ Clad 10¢ - (copper core bonded between copper/nickel layers) $2.<u>50</u>
- ◆ Clad 25¢ - (copper core bonded between copper/nickel layers) $4.<u>00</u>
- ◆ Clad 50¢ - (copper core bonded between copper/nickel layers) $18.<u>00</u>
- ◆ Clad Ike $1 - (copper core bonded between copper/nickel layers) $45.<u>00</u>
- ◆ Clad Anthony $1 - (copper core bonded between copper/nickel layers) $35.<u>00</u>

Not many forgers may feel inclined to use genuine wartime nickel or silver dollar planchets for their everyday forgery, but you have to admit that three dollars doesn't seem like much for them to be willing to spend in order to have a perfect planchet to strike an uncirculated 1877 or 1908-S Indian Head cent, a 1909-S VDB Lincoln, or a 1914-D, or even a 1955 double die. Likewise many will see $10 as a perfectly reasonable investment to make towards striking a 1916-D dime, and $5 could be considered a real bargain when it comes to doing nickels.

And as for clad coinage. . . well, while most clad issues aren't worth forging (there are one or two exceptions), clad planchets are often used for forging spectacular and valuable "mint errors" such as off centers, multiple strikes, brockages, and off metal strikes (wrong planchet, such as a dime struck as a cent). During one of my interviews a number of years ago with the forger Mark Hofmann, he described to me how as a

---

[1] Note: Alloy for " Indian Cent" is 1864-1909, and also applies to Lincoln cents1909-1942, 1947-1962. Alloy listed as "Lincoln Cent" applies to the slightly different composition of coins struck from 1944-1946 and 1962-1982.

teenager he used to create electroplate dies (see Chapter Five) of an uncirculated common coin, such as a quarter, and then use them to make multiple strike and off center errors, applying them to both ordinary coins and to blank planchets he had purchased. (Most of these forgeries are probably still in private collections in and around Salt Lake City, prized by their owners as legitimate mint errors.)

Because of this combination of availability, minor cost, and convenience; most struck forgeries of low denomination modern coins and errors are likely to be done on legitimate planchets. But there is a limit as to how practical this "source" can be to the forger. Obviously he won't be able to locate genuine blank planchets for a Massachusetts Pine Tree Shilling, or a piece of eight, or a half dime, or a quarter eagle — or for that matter, any gold coin at all. For quite a few coins, in fact, the forger's only recourse is to manufacture his own planchets.

Manufacturing Planchets — Machine-Struck Coinage

This can be a bit challenging to do just right, but it shouldn't be thought of as any more difficult than most of the other forgery techniques we've already discussed. A planchet, after all, is really nothing more than a plain, softened disc of metal. All the forger has to do is see to it that it contains the correct alloy, weighs what it is supposed to, is the right size and shape to be struck, and has the proper pre-striking finish on its surface. If he does, it will pass.

Since each of these things is important in its own way, we'll consider them separately:

Alloy

As a concerned and honest reader, lacking the larcenous thought processes of an actual forger, you may be wondering just how nit-picky a forger has to be about using exactly the right alloy. In one word, the answer is *very*. Along with weight, *alloy is the single most critical factor* of a planchet intended to be struck as a successful representation of a specific coin. This is because a coin's alloy — like its weight — can be precisely tested, either by measuring its specific gravity or, in some cases, by use of X-ray spectrography.

When a coin is submitted to a competent authentication service, its alloy simply will not remain a secret. Does a struck tetradrachm of Athens contain the appropriate trace elements one would expect to find in silver that was mined anciently in Attica, or does it consist of modern .900/.100 coin silver? Is a debased Roman *antoninianus* from the 3rd century composed of the correct proportions of lead, copper, tin, zinc, and silver for the particular decade in which it was minted? Or how about our gold dollars and quarter eagles from Chapter One — does their fineness match that of gold coins issued by the U.S. government during the second half of the 19th century, or is it the same as an ordinary Krugerrand? With the profit potential so high for a convincing product, and the risk of exposure so great for a slipshod one, I think we can safely say that the days are long gone when any forger would be careless or foolish enough to skimp on anything as basic as materials.

Besides, it just isn't that hard for them to come up with correct alloys. Information about the precise ratio of one metal to another within any given coin series is one of those technical tidbits that most avid numismatists are fond of knowing, and such data can easily be found within any number of printed references. And be assured that if we can look something up, so can a forger.

Let's say a forger intends to strike U.S. gold, for example. He will know that the date of the coins he plans to forge will naturally determine what alloy he uses, because a quick check in the *Red Book* will show him that gold coins issued from 1795-1834 contained .9167 parts gold to .0833 copper, those from 1834 to 1839-40 were .8992 parts gold to .1008 copper, and generally everything from 1840 on was .900 parts gold to .100 parts copper. If he is forging gold dollars (which were only struck from 1849-1889) he will need a gold/copper alloy that is 900 fine. If he is doing a quarter eagle from the scarce "Classic Head" series of 1834-1839, he will need one that is 899.225 fine. A 1799 eagle ($10) or an 1811 half eagle will require an alloy of 916 2/3 fineness. Admittedly these differences may not seem like much, but they are detectable, so the forger will want to match them.

Where will he get his alloy, you ask? One of two ways. He will either mix the alloy himself, weighing out portions of pure gold (from "Maple Leaf" or similar unalloyed bullion coins) with pieces of pure copper electrical wire and melting them together in a crucible (with a little flux, of course), or he can simply use the pre-mixed alloy of actual (but numismatically inferior) coins. Examples of the latter would be common date, heavily worn, holed or defaced specimens that often sell for scarcely more than their bullion value.

Certainly gold isn't the only alloy the forger can mix or collect, though. He can create custom silver alloys to do Spanish and English colonials or early American issues, melt down common date wheat cents to strike Indian Heads or early Lincolns, add copper to ordinary melted nickels to come up with the .880 copper/.120 nickel alloy used for the Flying Eagle and early Indian cents — in short, if he can look it up, he can produce it.

Weight

There really isn't much to say about weight that isn't already obvious. Not only can the weight of a coin be accurately measured, it is usually the first and probably the easiest type of test made, and can be performed by anyone. About the only thing a forger has to remember is that the weight of his forged coin will be whatever the weight of his planchet is, so if he takes care to get the one right, the other will fall right into place.

Size and Shape

Or to be more precise, "How Planchets Are Made". We'll look at two methods here, both of which apply to planchets used for modern, machine struck-coinage types. (I'll be covering planchets for hammer-struck coinage, both ancient and medieval, separately a little later on.)

The first method, called *swedging*, is actually very similar to the coinage process itself. It involves pressure forming a pre-weighed cast lump of alloy between two specially prepared swedging dies within a collar well, forming a flat, perfectly round planchet. In essence, swedging is the minting of a "blank coin" which can then be struck *as* a coin. The tool used to create planchets by swedging is almost identical to the simple, three-piece device described and shown in Chapter Five in the section on *hubbing*. There are just a couple of differences to mention.

If the coin is to be struck within a collar, rather than broadstruck, then for the planchet to be able to fit into the minting collar the diameter of the swedging collar well must be slightly less — say, a hundredth of an inch or so for most small to medium sized coins — than the finished coin will be. Also, the planchet will need to have an *upset edge*, which is a slightly thickened area around the outside of a planchet that helps the metal flow more easily up into the rim area of a coining die during minting. This type of edge is usually rolled onto a cut out disc of metal by a device quite like the edge marking machine described in the last chapter, only using plain die strips instead of lettered or ornamented ones. In the case of swedged planchets, though, it is just as easy to achieve the same effect by machining a slightly curved rim into the edges of the anvil and trussel dies.

The face of a planchet-forming swedging die with a slight incuse groove at its edge. This produces a planchet with a satisfactory "upset edge" for minting a coin with a conventional rim.

To swedge a planchet, the forger will first carefully weigh out a pile of chips, grains, and particles of his alloy until he has the exact weight he needs, and then melt the mass into a single, solid lump. This lump is then placed between the dies inside the collar well, and the dies are smacked repeatedly with a hammer until the planchet is formed.

Needless to say, the metal being swedged must be extremely ductile in order to flow into and fill the entire space between the dies without cracking in the process. The high gold alloys normally used for coinage work very well this way, and swedging is an ideally simple and convenient method for creating gold planchets up to about the size of a five dollar gold piece. Other metals such as silver and copper may also be swedged effectively, but as they will stress harden with striking they require frequent annealing before the planchet is completed. The best non-gold results are achieved with smaller coins such as the silver three cent pieces, half dimes and dimes, or the cent, but anything much larger will have too much difficulty flowing well using mere hammer pressure — no matter how often it is annealed.

But the necessity of annealing the metal so many times during the swedging of non-gold alloys also creates a problem with weight control, which the forger must anticipate and compensate for.

Suppose, for instance, a forger set out to make a planchet to strike a nice 1864 Indian cent with the L on the hair ribbon (composition 95% copper, 2 1/2% tin, 2 1/2% zinc; uncirculated weight 3.11 grams). Any other cent minted up through 1942, or from 1947-1961 would provide the exact same alloy and weight he wants, so in theory he should be able to just melt down another cent and swedge a planchet from it, right?

Well, let's say he tries just that. He selects a 1959-D and melts it into an amorphous blob, quenching it when it solidifies (but while it is still red-hot) in order to anneal it. So far, so good. Heating the metal red-hot will have caused its surface molecules to combine with oxygen in the air, however, so his quench will likely consist of a mild acidic pickling solution that will remove this heat scale and leave a clean surface. Each time the forger heats the metal while annealing it this scale will form, and each time it will be removed during the quench. When the metal has finally taken the final form of a finished planchet, he will anneal and clean it a final time, in preparation for striking in his dies.

But first he will want to check the weight of his planchet — and guess what? It now weighs somewhat less than the 3.11 grams it started out with.

You know what happened, of course. Each pickling removed the scale, but it also removed the surface molecules that combined with oxygen to make up the scale in the first place. One or two annealings won't have much effect, but several add up. The forger deals with this situation easily, though, by simply adding whatever amount of alloy he calculates he has lost during his "test run" to all subsequent batches he starts out with. Copper and silver alloys will both lose measurable amounts of weight over the course of the swedging process. Gold, which does not oxidize, will lose none.

The second method of planchet making is basically just a scaled-down version of the same process used by mints. The forger will melt and cast his alloy into a small bar or ingot, pass it several times through a pair of steel rollers to reduce it to plate, punch out circular blanks from this plate, and then either mark or upset their edges on an edge marking machine.

There are some singular advantages to this method over swedging, particularly for the forger working with non-gold alloys. Planchets of any size can be cut, for instance, and the thickness of the plate can be adjusted and set to allow precise weight control of the blanks as they are punched out. Since the plate's thickness is determined by its final pass through the rollers just prior to punching, the several annealings and cleanings the strip will undergo have no effect at all on the final weight of the blanks that are cut from it. This means that once the weight of a planchet has been established (by punching it out), it will only have to be annealed and cleaned one time before being struck. But possibly the greatest advantage to this process is that once the forger has it all set up he can adapt it to create as few or as many planchets at a time as he wishes, and they will always be identical.

About the only real disadvantage is that it requires a couple more pieces of specialized equipment.

The first item the forger will need, obviously, is a metal plate roller. Real mints nowadays have enormous ones, with several sets of huge rollers and built-in annealing furnaces along the line, which can put out a continuous strip of alloy around the clock, stretching all the way from the melting crucibles to the punching presses.

The device a forger will use is almost quaint by comparison — but make no mistake; it is just as effective for his purposes, and can duplicate the effects he wants perfectly. He will need a bench mounted, adjustable jeweler's plate roller, which is slightly smaller than an old-fashioned washing machine wringer, and operates exactly the same way. The forger can acquire one through a jewelry manufacturing supply source or, if he chooses, can construct one of his own design without too much difficulty in the privacy of his workshop on his lathe.

Operating a small plate roller such as this is simple, provided the metal being rolled is annealed enough to be ductile. The amount of compression that can be applied in a single pass will depend largely on the size of the rollers and the ratio of the drive gears, but generally alloys of copper or silver will be reduced only a slight amount for one or two passes before annealing, cleaning, and rolling again. The forger merely keeps repeating this process until he has achieved the exact plate thickness which, when punched out to form a blank of a specific diameter, will give him a planchet of the weight he wants. With experimentation and a few trial runs, he can determine the right thickness quite easily.

A small bench mounted, adjustable jeweler's plate roller — an unusual item for most home workshops, but not particularly difficult to obtain.

Next, the forger will need a punch and die set in order to cut the blanks out with, and since the planchets for each type of coin he forges will be a different size, these tools will have to be custom made.

I should probably mention here that I've come across a number of accounts about how this process — known as *blanking* — is supposed to be done in actual mints, and the comparison that seems to be made most often is to a "cookie cutter". Unfortunately, that's not only an oversimplified way of describing it, it's also inaccurate. I know what a punch and die set looks like, and frankly I've never seen a punch and die that resembles a cookie cutter, or for that matter, a cookie cutter that works like a punch and die. A cookie cutter *cuts* through dough, like a geometrically shaped knife, while a punch and die *shears* material by pushing it through a sharp-edged hole. If you've ever used a paper hole punch, you've used a punch and die.

Almost nothing is easier to make. The *die* consists of a block of steel with a hole in the top of it that is the exact size the punched out blank will be. This hole goes all the way through the steel block, and is often relieved to a slightly larger diameter (for clearance and removal of punchings) from about half an inch in from the opening on down. The corner where the edge of the hole meets the upper surface should be clean, flat, and sharp. The *punch* is no more than a flat faced, sharp cornered steel rod turned to a diameter that will just fit inside the hole, and is long enough to hold on to and whack with a hammer. Both the punch and the die are hardened and tempered for use, of course.

A typical homemade punch and die for blanking. Note the strip of schissel.

The trick to using it is to be able to center the punch directly over the hole in the die, while at the same time the hole is covered up with a piece of alloy plate waiting to be punched. The forger will waste a lot of time trying to do this freehand, for it cannot be done without the aid of some sort of guide. One method would be to arrange a "punch well" in a fixed location over the die, with an open space on the bottom of it that would allow the strip of alloy plate to be inserted. Another way would be to construct the entire die about three-quarters of an inch thicker, and cut a horizontal slot part way through it (but *all* the way through the hole) for the plate to be slipped into. A clever forger will undoubtedly figure out something.

Blanking punch and die separated, showing construction and collection chamber. The forger will find that these work with less effort when the punch and well parts are sprayed with a Teflon-type lubricant during use.

Relatively small blanks can be successfully punched with hammer power alone, but medium size to larger blanks will require more striking force to shear them from the thicker plate they are made from than can usually be managed with a mere hand held hammer. The forger may possibly accomplish this with something similar to an arbor press, or with one of the minting devices discussed in the next chapter. (By the way, the common term for the leftover plate after the blanks have been punched from it is *schissel*. I'm not really sure why. That's just what it's always been called.)

Blanks to be made into planchets that will be struck within collars next need to receive their upset edge, where they are slightly compressed and thickened all around their circumference by being rolled between two plain, unmarked die strips in an edge marking machine (see Chapter Seven). This will also reduce the diameter of the blank — which typically starts out around .005" larger than the finished coin diameter — to a new size that is .005" smaller than the coin (so that the planchet can fit inside the collar to be struck).[2]

---

[2] When blanks are edge marked to receive incuse lettering in order to be struck in a plain collar, this also produces an upset edge around the planchet.

An upset edge may also be easily applied to planchets by constructing a small edge-rolling machine, similar to this one. Not a difficult project at all.

Pre-Striking Finish

Any collector who has ever examined a bright, shiny uncirculated coin (and who hasn't?) is aware of three things: the sharpness of the detail on the coin types; the clean, brilliant appearance of the surface; and the simple fact that, unless care is taken to protect the coin, both of these qualities begin to deteriorate rather quickly. What this means to a forger is that coins start out crisp and shiny because the planchets they were struck on started out soft and clean.

(One interesting note here: While bright, shiny new coins might be asthetically pleasing, this is not the reason official mints have historically gone to all the trouble of making them that way for everyday business strikes. A "dirty" planchet is basically covered with a thin layer of very abrasive oxidation, which will erode the working surfaces of dies just as an aluminum-oxide grinding wheel can wear away steel.)

Planchets are always, *always* annealed before they are struck into coins, whether they are silver, copper, brass, bronze, nickel — and even gold.

Annealing, which we've talked about a number of times already, has the effect of "loosening" the mechanical bonds within the crystalline molecular structure of an alloy, making it as malleable as possible. The softer a planchet is, the less force is required from the dies to bring up a crisp, clear image. Dies hold up longer, and provide more strikes — an especially important point to forgers, who will often be using the less substantial dies created by plating, casting, or hubbing, rather than dies made of steel. Planchets for broadstruck coins generally were annealed prior to receiving their edge marking; planchets for collar struck coins are always annealed after the upset edge is applied.

Real mints now use inert gas atmosphere electric annealing furnaces, but unless the forger has access to one he will end up having to clean his planchets (except for gold ones) after annealing them. A mildly acidic pickling bath is effective for removing light scale, but can leave the surface of the alloy looking "frosted" and off color. The forger's solution, again, is to do what real mints do and "polish" them by gently tumbling a quantity of them together for several hours (or overnight) in a small, rubber-lined lapidary rock tumbler. A handful of clean silica sand and a little cream of tartar will help the process along, provided the finished planchets are afterward rinsed with distilled water and dried before they are struck.

Manufacturing Planchets — Hammer-Struck Coinage

The forger who takes on the task of duplicating planchets for ancient, medieval, and later hammer-struck coinage issues will find his job a great deal simpler and at the same time far more challenging than creating planchets for modern coins. The mechanical processes involved in fabricating a pre-mechanized product are easy to learn and employ, but the duplication of precise alloy — for which there is little accurate information available — can be a real headache.

When a forger wants to reproduce an obsolete alloy from the mechanized period, he usually has only to look it up somewhere. He will find that Bath metal,[3] for instance, is composed of 75% copper, 24.7% zinc, and .03% silver, and proceed accordingly to mix it up. But when he tries to create Roman *orichalcum* — a brass alloy consisting of about 80 parts copper to 20 parts zinc, used for both the *dupondius* and the *sestertius* —

---

3 Used by English coiner William Wood for his unpopular *Rosa Americana* series.

he runs up against the problem of inheriting more technology than the Romans possessed. Ancient refining processes were imperfect, and their alloys were often poorly mixed, or contained impurities that metallurgists were either incapable of removing or considered too much trouble to bother with. These "impurities" were actually small traces of other metals, which varied in composition and ratio with the particular ores they originated from. Even when approximate proportions of an alloy were recorded, as with orichalcum, the exact composition remains unknown to all but the select few who have examined Roman coins using X-ray spectrography.

Carl Wilhelm Becker (see Chapter Five), who lived long before such modern examination tools were even dreamed of, seems to have hit upon the only practical answer without ever realizing how crucial to successful forgery the issue would one day become. Just as many modern forgers use modern coins as an accurate alloy source, Becker used heavily worn, holed, and defaced *ancients* as a source for his planchets! Becker never drempt that minor variations in alloy composition could lead to the possibility of detection; He simply found the numismatically inferior specimens to be "convenient" for him to use.

Given the limited number of surviving ancients — even those in poor condition — would a modern forger actually resort to the same thing? With the profit potential what it is, I suspect he would easily. His only other recourse is research and trial and error.

So let's say that the forger has his alloy on hand and is ready to convert it into a blank planchet. For most ancients, all he has to do is weigh it out, melt it, and cast it as a thick disc. Some planchets were simply "puddled" on a flat surface; some were contained around their edges and given shape in strip metal forms; some were cast in terra-cotta or sandstone molds. Some were cast with side sprue channels, which had to be either cut or broken off, and some were cast in strips all connected to each other, and were later separated. Some were quite irregular, while others were fairly uniform. Some even appear to have been pre-shaped a bit with a hammer before being struck. The forger will study as many examples and photographs of original coins as he can, attempt to discover what particular processes were used, and experiment until he has duplicated them. Once the research has been done, however, the actual techniques aren't difficult at all.

Medieval (and later) hammer-struck planchets go just a step beyond ancients, and are even easier to reproduce. Without having to worry about whatever specific casting techniques were originally used, a lump of alloy is simply beaten with a hammer (but *not* rolled! Plate rolling technology didn't appear until the early part of the sixteenth century.) upon a flat surface to produce a thin, flat plate.

Earliest medieval planchets seem to have been made by cutting this plate with snips into rough squares, which were then struck between the coinage dies. If the strike was considered good, and adequately centered on both sides, the coin was then cut from the square using a circular-centered chisel (which, coincidentally, *does* resemble a cookie cutter!).[4] Later on, planchets were made more quickly by cutting them out using snips or chisels prior to striking them. Many of these planchets were also adjusted for weight by the mint by trimming their edges with a chisel. (Small wonder clipping was such a common problem.)

Finally, some planchets were first cast by weight into "pellets" and then flattened with a hammer to make a more or less round disc of metal, a concept not at all unlike the forger's technique of swedging pre-weighed pellets into workable planchets (but without the collar, naturally).

Thin planchets were annealed and cleaned prior to striking, but many large, thick ancients with extremely high relief had to be *hot struck*. This process involved heating the cast planchets to just before the glow point (about 1000° F.), placing them between the dies using tongs, and giving them a good whack to begin to "set" the detail. Since it is next to impossible to reposition a hot planchet, these partially struck coins were usually then annealed, cleaned, and finished by cold striking.

Now that we're beginning to get into minting practices, we might as well go all the way. I've shown you how forgers can create dies, make collars, do edge marking, and come up with convincing planchets. I think we're finally ready to take a look at how the actual forgeries are made.

---

[4] A perfect example of this can be seen with the silver pennies of the Anglo-Saxon king Aethelred II (978-1016 A.D.). A few coins struck on untrimmed planchets have managed to survive — all of which are so poorly done as to appear to be rejects.

Chapter Nine

Minting Machinery and Processes

Every numismatist is, to a greater or lesser degree, a custodian of history. They — with the possible exception of those few who see coins merely as investments and think mostly in terms of price trends and condition appraisals — are concerned not only with the preservation of the artifacts temporarily in their care, but with enlarging our understanding of them, and of the people who created and used them. An important part of this experience, which has always been of intense interest, is the study of how coins are made.

Forgers share this quest for information, though of course with a different object in mind. By learning or speculating about how a certain thing was done, they are able to form theories for which they develop hypotheses, which they test by experiment after experiment until, finally, they hit upon a method that will duplicate the effect they are seeking. The truth boils down to the fact that the only people who really understand as much about coin making methods as the people who make coins — are forgers.

You've seen the way this happens a number of times already. A forger wants to make a reeded collar; he finds out how reeded collars are made and copies the process. A forger needs a planchet with an upset edge; he either scales down the same method the mint uses or duplicates the effect an entirely different way. A forger wants accurate dies; he appropriates the images from actual coins, using a variety of unorthodox and ingenious approaches.

It is no different with minting practices. The forger begins with a developed understanding of the techniques originally used, and either imitates or modifies them to suit his own needs. The alternatives and options available to him in doing so are practically endless, of course, but the following examples should give some idea of what a knowledgeable forger with average resources is capable of.

A contemporary illustration of coinmaking in the fifteenth century. (From the Spiez Chronicle of Diebold Schilling, Bern 1486 - Burgerbibliothek, Bern.)

Hammered Coinage

Hammer striking is undeniably the simplest method of coin making imaginable. A blank planchet, placed upon a lower die, is covered with an upper die, which is then struck with a hammer from one to several times. That's it. Nearly all Western coinage during the first 2,000 years of its existence was manufactured this way. But was it actually as easy to do as it sounds?

In some cases yes, and in some cases no. If all we had to judge by were illustrations from contemporary medieval manuscripts, we'd probably think that everything from *pfennigs* to *Joachmsthalers* could be knocked out in nothing flat by a couple of casual taps from a ridiculously small hammer. But it doesn't quite work that way.

A coin die is really just a broad punch, which has to be driven into the metal it strikes. The larger the surface area of the punch, the more force is required to make an impression — and since coin dies are used in pairs and have to impress both sides of a planchet at the same time, the force needed can be considerable for all but the very smallest of coins.

Dime-size coins — such as the sigloi shown here[1] — could usually be struck by a single person holding the upper die in one hand and swinging

A number of silver Persian Sigloi, shown with a gold Daric (the more round coin of the group). These coins are approximately the size of a dime, but about three times as thick.

[1] Note: The reproduction Persian sigloi (c. 5th century B.C.) in the photograph are not actual forgeries, though their method of manufacture is in every respect identical to that used for the better class of numismatic forgery. Shown are legally produced replicas, marked and published as such, struck with hand engraved dies. (Photo courtesy of The Ancient Mint.)

a 3-pound sledgehammer with the other. While it is also possible to strike somewhat larger coins single-handedly this way, we should bear in mind that the tendency to flinch is an instinctive form of self-preservation. The harder the swing, the more likely one is to flinch, so to do so well requires quite a bit of practice and skill.

In order to be able to generate the force necessary for striking the much larger coins (the Greek *decadrachm*, or the Roman *sestertius*, for example), two people were needed — one of them to hold the upper die in place with a constant downward bearing pressure, and the other to swing a heavy sledge with both hands while trying to hit it squarely on. This required even greater skill, and inexperience or fatigue could cause serious damage to one's assistant.

Few forgers are likely to find such agreeable (and expendable) assistants, though, and most will prefer to work alone in any case. What a forger will have to do is substitute inventiveness to make up for his shortcomings in skill, experience, and manpower. He does this by constructing a jig to hold both the upper and lower dies in position while he strikes them. In essence, he builds a simple hammer-striking machine.

The device illustrated is a good example of the sort of thing we're talking about. It consists of a good, sturdy base (A) made from a piece of 1" thick

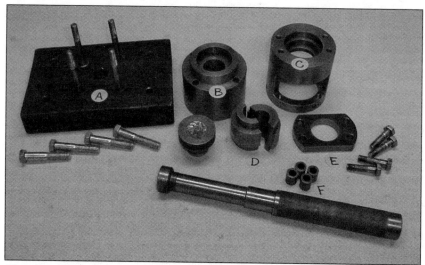

The various parts of a homemade simple hammer-striking machine. Note the long trussel handle affixed to the upper die; it is knurled to assure that a non-slip grasp can be maintained while applying downward pressure.

plate steel; a lower die holder (B) and an upper die mount (C), which are machined to fit together; a bronze split bushing (D) which fits into the upper die mount and is bored to accommodate the shaft of the upper die; and a hold-down plate (E) and some spacer washers (F).

The base, lower die holder, and upper die mount are all joined by four machine bolts passing up from underneath, while the split bushing is kept in place by the hold-down plate, which is bolted to the top of the upper die mount. The upper die is fixed to the lower end of a thick steel rod, which forms a shaft sticking up through the split bushing, and is long enough to be able to grasp with one hand while swinging a hammer to strike it with the other. On either side of the upper die mount are openings to allow easy access to the area where the two dies meet, so that planchets can be inserted and removed without having to disassemble everything.

A simple jig like this will hold the upper die in constant vertical alignment with the lower die, overcoming the effect of the striker's urge to flinch.

With the base firmly bolted to a sturdy, shock absorbent pedestal, all the forger has to do is lift the upper die shaft, place a blank planchet (whether hot or cold) between the die faces, and hold on to the die shaft with a firm downward pressure while striking the top of it with a hammer. It is much easier to deliver

Simple hammer-striking machine in use. Since it has no moving parts, this device is actually more of a jig than a machine.

more forceful blows this way than by attempting to hold the upper die freehanded, because the forger knows that the striking area will not waver or move, even involuntarily.

The only difficulty lies with the need to constantly grasp the upper die shaft to apply downward pressure while striking. Not only is this awkward and tiring, but it still leaves the forger's hand and wrist in uncomfortable proximity to the sledgehammer's target. This problem can be easily overcome, though, with the addition of a downward pressure lever to the device.

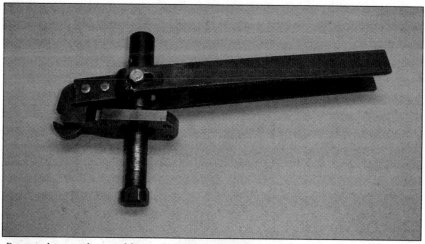

Downward pressure lever modification. Note the shortening of the trussel.

By replacing the plain hold-down plate with one that has been modified with a built-in lug on one end, a hooked lever can be attached to the jig. The lever shown in the photograph splits where it joins at this hook, forming two bars that extend horizontally along either side of the upright die shaft. A pair of bolts pass through slots cut through the sides of these bars and thread directly into the die shaft, forming "trunnions" for the lever to bear against.

When the forger bears down against the end of this lever, quite a bit of downward pressure can comfortably be developed to keep the upper die in contact with the planchet, which will in turn prevent the coin from shifting and becoming misaligned during striking. The forger can now rain repeated blows upon the top of the die shaft with far more force than he might have dared when he felt his hand might become a casualty.

Simple hammer-striking machine with downward pressure lever in use.

But it's still hard work. And even though the forger can effectively strike medium-sized coins this way, larger coins or coins with excessively high relief just cannot be struck well single-handedly. He could employ an assistant to bear down on the lever (or accomplish the same thing with an arrangement of springs) while he swings a double-handed sledge — but this too is hard work.

It's also unnecessary, because one further modification can provide him with all the striking force he could ever want or need.

With the addition of a connecting sleeve and a length of steel pipe to serve as a drop guide, an overhead pulley wheel, some rope, and a large bar of steel for a hammer, the forger can construct a true minting machine called a *gravity hammer.*

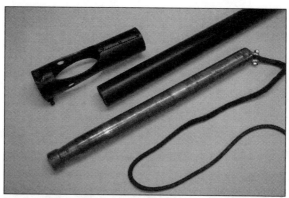

Parts for gravity hammer adaptation.

Gravity hammers represent one of the first mechanical improvements over hand-hammered coinage methods, and were in use during the first half of the 16th century by the central European Germanic states to mint large, multiple units of the silver thaler. They are slow to use (one of the main reasons they were generally replaced by other minting methods) and the shock stress they produce can be rather hard on dies, but they are relatively simple to build, easy to operate, take up little space, and are capable of generating enormous force — all factors which make them ideally suited for numismatic forgery.

The gravity hammer shown in the photos has a hammer guide that extends through the ceiling to a pulley mounted near the ceiling of the room above it, and is capable of dropping a 32 lb. hammer for a distance of twelve feet onto the top of a die shaft 1" in diameter. I'm not going to bother to do the math, but let it suffice to say that the striking force it can generate is easily enough to mint a coin the size of a silver dollar. The assortment of silver Athenian tetradrachms[2] in the photo (opposite page) — coins which have extremely high relief detail — were all successfully struck on this very machine.

By simply varying the distance he pulls the rope in order to raise the hammer before releasing it, the forger has complete control over the amount of force that will be produced for each strike. By raising the hammer to the same place, he can also duplicate his striking force consistently. Thus, with a knowledge of historic minting methods and a bit of adaptive inventiveness, the forger can create a simple machine to replicate with ease the effects of virtually any size of hammer-struck coin.

[2] See previous footnote. (Photo courtesy of The Ancient Mint.)

Left: Lower portion of gravity hammer machine.
Right: Upper pulley arrangement for gravity hammer machine.

Silver Athenian tetradrachms.

Contemporary illustration of a screw press in use, from Diderot's Encyclopedie, 1771.

But what can he do about the more modern types of coins that were originally struck by machines?

Practically anything he wants. But first, a little background. . .

Machine-Struck Coinage

When people during the Renaissance began experimenting with mechanical methods of imparting force to a pair of coin dies, the eventual end of hammer striking became a foregone conclusion. Gravity hammers offered one option, but they were quickly replaced as soon as faster, more efficient methods evolved. The development of plate rollers, for example, spawned in some places the idea of engraving die faces directly onto the steel roller cylinders in order to impress rows of coin images onto a strip of plate during its final pass, which could be separately punched out afterward. In practice it was difficult to achieve perfectly round images this way, however, and weight control was always a problem.

Most areas ultimately adopted the *screw press*, a highly successful minting machine which harnessed the centrifugal force of a spinning, weighted arm in order to turn a vertical screw and drive coin dies together. Powered first by human muscle, and later by steam, screw presses "squeezed" planchets into coins with a relatively slow, steady force that was quite easy on dies. Virtually all broadstruck coins with ornamented edges were minted on such machines.

Screw presses continued to be the preferred means of striking coins well on into the 19th century, when they finally began to be supplanted by the *knuckle press*, which harnessed steam power more effectively. Driven now by electricity, the descendants of the basic knuckle press are still in wide use today.

Contemporary illustration of a knuckle press, from Harper's Magazine, December 1861.

All of which is very interesting to most of us, but other than providing useful background information, it means very little to a forger. Aside from the few more esoteric methods of mechanical coin production — such as the roller press described briefly above (which is so exotic and of limited use that we won't bother to get into forgeries of its method here) — all machine produced coins had one basic element in common: they were *struck*. When you disregard such factors as speed and efficiency, any one form of striking is capable of producing results very much like any other form of striking.

Nothing prevents a forger from acquiring or constructing a screw press if he wants to — and I'm sure that somewhere along the line there have been some who have done just that — but the fact is that any screw press large enough to generate adequate minting force takes up quite a bit of space, and would be difficult for a person working alone to operate. (Actually, the same "squeezing" effect produced by a screw press can be readily duplicated with a simple arbor press consisting of little more than a sturdy framework and a 20-ton hydraulic jack. The employment of such a basic device is so self-explanatory that we needn't take the space to cover it here.)

A forger can also put together a knuckle press if he so desires, though they are large, complicated, expensive, and designed for speed and capacity that the forger has no need of. The basic issue returns to the need for a device that is simple to build, easy to operate, takes up little space, and is capable of generating enormous force.

Once again, the gravity hammer appears to provide the most reasonable solution.

The gravity hammer already shown needs very little modification to allow it to produce machine-struck coinage; in fact, with properly configured dies it can do broadstriking exactly as it is. If the forger plans to strike planchets within a collar, though, there are a couple of things he will need to do first, such as figuring out how he will mount the collar and coming up with a way to eject the freshly struck forgeries from it. Much of this will depend upon how he shapes his finished dies to work within the machine. There are obviously a great many ways to do so, but I think we can illustrate the point perfectly well by simply taking a look at how it was done for this particular one.

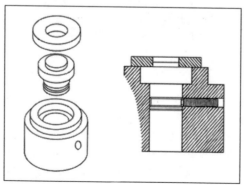

Configuration of lower die and means of installation in lower die holder. Die axis is set by simply rotating the lower die and tightening the set screw.

There is a die well in the lower die holder that is basically just a stepped hole, the upper part being 1-5/8" in diameter and 1/2" deep, and the lower 1" in diameter and extending all the way through to the bottom of the holder. Interchangeable lower dies are machined to slip into this hole and lie flush with the upper surface of the die holder. The 1" diameter protrusion on the bottom of the lower die contains a recessed groove which lines up with a threaded hole in the side of the holder. This allows a set screw to lock the die into position once it has been rotated to achieve its desired orientation with the upper die, or its proper *die axis*.

The window-like openings on the sides of the upper die mount are large enough to allow lower dies to be inserted and dropped into place, but getting them out again is a different matter. The entire apparatus will need to be disassembled, and the base plate unbolted from its pedestal in order to turn the lower die holder upside-down each time the forger wants to change dies — unless he installs some means of raising the lower die up from within the holder. This is easy enough to do by installing a simple lever/piston arrangement on the pedestal, as shown here.

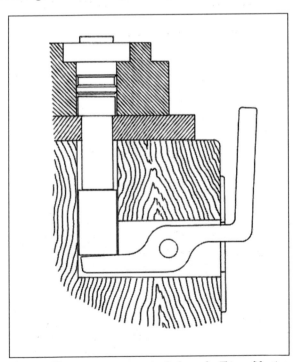

Piston and lever arrangement to raise the lower die. This modification is built into the pedestal that the minting machine is mounted to.

A slight pressure on this lever will raise the small piston beneath the base of the minting machine, pushing the lower die up from within its well. This feature will also be useful for ejecting freshly struck coins from plain and reeded collars, as you will see in a moment.

Back in Chapter Seven, I mentioned that dies used with collars require a sharply defined neck to allow the die face to enter the opening of the collar. This neck, for the lower die, should in all cases be as deep as the collar is thick, which is about twice the thickness of the planchet for medium to larger coins, and three or four times the thickness for smaller coins.

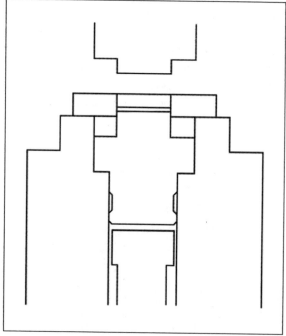

Use of lever to raise lower die to eject coin from collar. Note that the die is set approximately ¼" lower in the die holder than previously, and the neck of the striking surface is also higher by the same amount (to bring it within the collar for striking). The collar will have to be firmly affixed to the die holder to use this adaptation.

When set up properly for striking, the face of the lower die will protrude up into the collar for about 1/2 of a coin thickness, so that when the upper die (which also is machined with a sharply defined neck) is brought down against the planchet laying on top of the lower die, both die faces are slightly within the collar. This will mean that, if the edge of the collar is to rest on top of the rim of the lower die holder, the surface of the lower die face must be raised slightly higher than the level of the holder rim. The forger can accomplish this height adjustment for his lower die by machining a thin, free-fitting shim washer to rest between the shoulder of the die well and the base of the die. (Note: since this shoulder is the area where all of the force of the hammer is arrested, it is important that this shim washer be made of properly hardened steel.)

The edge of the collar, as mentioned, rests on top of the rim of the lower die holder. By drilling and tapping two holes for small bolts in the rim of the holder, and machining corresponding holes or notches on the collar, the forger can easily secure the collar in place for striking. The die raising lever can then be used to push the die face up level to the top of the collar, effectively ejecting the struck coin.

Segmented collars can also be used with this gravity hammer arrangement in exactly the same way, but of course they will need to be removed and disassembled to release the coins that are struck in them.

When using the gravity hammer, it will always be necessary for the forger to use one hand to bear down upon the pressure lever for the upper die. This is because the hammer has a tendency to "bounce" after hitting the top of the upper die shaft, and without adequate pressure the planchet can bounce along with it, causing a doubled image on the strike. To free his other hand for placing planchets and other tasks, the forger may even want to rig up some sort of automatic release for the hammer rope, which he can trip with his foot.

Doubtless there are many such modifications he could continue to make in the name of greater convenience, all based upon his perceived needs and his inventiveness.

The simple gravity hammer just described can produce enough force to mint a Syracuse decadrachm, a seated Liberty dollar, or a piece of eight with almost equal ease, as well as anything smaller. It is uncomplicated to build, easy to operate, and takes up little space — but it isn't very portable. For striking forgeries of the smaller coins, many forgers may feel that they would prefer to make and use something that is even simpler.

Hammer-Striking Machine-Struck Coinage

When we talked about creating dies by hubbing a while back, I showed you a little three-piece tool that I called "an extremely simple form of a portable, hammer-striking minting machine," and promised I'd be showing you a slightly more versatile version a little later on. Well, the gravity hammer wasn't what I meant. This is.

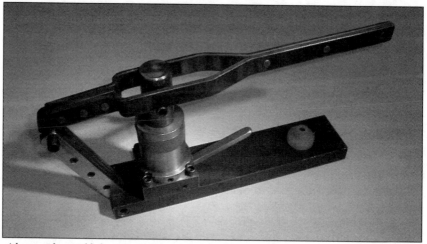

A homemade portable hammer-striking minting machine.

As you can see, the three main components of the basic hubbing device shown back in Chapter Five — the *anvil, trussel,* and *well* — are still obvious as the main parts of the machine, but they have been modified here just a bit to be a great deal more useful.

The anvil has now become a lower die holder, similar to but slightly smaller than the one used with the gravity hammer, which will also accept the same size and shape of interchangeable lower dies. The trussel, rather than being turned to the same diameter as the finished coin, is now a larger, thicker affair with a threaded base to accept interchangeable upper dies — just as the upper die shaft on the gravity hammer does. And the guide well, which no longer functions as a collar as it did with the hubbing device, screws onto the lower die holder and is bored to accept the trussel with a snug yet freely-moving fit. A shoulder inside the lower opening of the guide well is turned to provide space to accommodate the use of a collar which, when used, rests directly on the rim of the lower die. Die axis control is again obtained by rotating the lower die and securing it with a set screw, since the upper die (as on the gravity hammer) is non-adjustable when screwed into the trussel. Orientation of the trussel, meanwhile, is maintained by the end of a guide screw threaded through the side of the well which rides along a vertical groove cut into the trussel's side.

A blank planchet being placed within the collar.

Also as with the gravity hammer, a downward pressure lever is used to bear against a pair of trunnions on the side of the trussel during striking in order to prevent the planchet from slipping or becoming misaligned. Finally, the lower die holder is bolted to one end of a sturdy steel base, which is just long enough to counterbalance the force applied to the pressure lever so that the machine will not fall over.

Using it is really quite simple. The forger first installs the lower die and adjusts it to its desired die axis position. He then places a collar (if used) on top of it with the die face protruding slightly up into the collar's opening. A blank planchet is then placed in the collar, and the trussel guide well screwed onto the lower die holder. (There should be a slight gap between the top of the collar and the shoulder inside the guide well so that they do not actually touch, in order to avoid the possibility of even slightly twisting the collar and damaging the fresh strike when unscrewing the well afterward.) The trussel, with the upper die already secured to it, is gently slipped into the well and allowed to rest against the planchet, and the detachable downward pressure lever installed. All the forger has to do now is bear down on the lever and whack the top of the trussel with a single-handed sledgehammer.

The trussel well unscrewed, revealing a freshly minted 1943 copper cent.

There is no provision for raising the lower die on this machine, so to eject the freshly struck coin the forger merely removes the pressure lever, pulls out the trussel, unscrews the well, and lifts up the collar. The coin can then be pushed out of the collar by pressing it squarely against the end of a short piece of wooden dowel.

A forger with a good arm can easily develop enough force on a machine this size to strike silver coins as large as a dime, copper cents, or even gold coins up to the size of an eagle ($10). As a matter of fact, a number of the mid-19th century California private gold issues are believed to have been hammer-struck, possibly using a device very similar to this one. With care, the results can be as fine as any produced by regular minting equipment.

On a simple, portable hammer-striking minting machine such as this, with a good set of nickel dies made by electroplating (Chapter Five), a reeded collar produced by broaching (Chapter Seven), and a pile of swedged gold planchets (Chapter Eight), our larcenous-minded forger could sit at his kitchen table watching television and knock out the forged gold coins mentioned in Chapter One all day long, anytime he wanted to.

Which would be wrong, of course — though I doubt such a thought is going to stop him.

The finished coin is removed from the collar by pressing it out against a small, nylon post set onto the base of the machine.

Chapter Ten

Wear, Aging, and Patina

As I sit writing this, I am holding a nickel that I just fished out of my pocket a little while ago. I've been listening to it tell me the story of its life.

No, I haven't been messing around with the old "tricky tobacco", and I am quite sober, thanks just the same. I think that every coin collector with any sort of imagination at all knows exactly what I'm talking about, though.

The faint scratch I can see on Jefferson's cheek, for example — that was put there in the summer of '63 when ten-year-old Marty Slobicki dropped some of his money in the street while waiting for his turn to buy a popsicle from the Good Humor man. (His older sister Judy immediately put her foot over it, and he had to punch her in the arm to get her to move.) More than thirty years of being passed from hand to hand and pocket to pocket has nearly worn the scratch away, but it's still visible — and no other nickel in the world has one exactly like it.

So it is with all coins, each having its own, individual history written upon its surfaces, unique from all others. One spent its entire existence laying in a bag in the basement of a Federal Reserve bank in Chicago, while another traveled for years before finally retiring to rest half-buried in the sand on a beach near Santa Monica. Still others were mired among the rotting timbers of shipwrecks, or tossed down wishing wells, or cast indifferently aside by a Sioux woman searching the pockets of the dead after the Battle of the Little Big Horn, or run over in an alley by the tires of a Model A Ford. Every nick, every ding, every mark and scratch tells a different story, which is a large part of the allure of coin collecting.

But does such sentimental romanticism mean anything at all to the mercenary heart of a forger? It most certainly does. The aspect of unique individuality is just one more part of a coin's fabric that he must attempt to successfully forge. Not only that, he must also attempt to obscure all evidence of any such distinctiveness that may have been passed on from the original master coin he appropriated his images from to his own

Numismatic Forgery

creations. He will do this by artificially reproducing the effects of random contact marks, circulation wear, aging, and patina.

A random contact mark is simply something like the scratch on Marty's nickel. Practically every coin in a grade lower than MS-63 (choice uncirculated) has a few, some more or less noticeable than others. If our forger is striking his coins from dies made by any of the "image appropriation" methods we've discussed (plating, casting, hubbing, or explosive impact), the forgeries will not only bear faithful duplications of the original coin's types, but also of its imperfections — including its random contact marks.

Marty's nickel happens to be a 1962-D, which no forger with any sense would ever waste his time copying. But let's just say it was — oh. . . a 1943-P, 3 over 2 wartime nickel. If the forger could avoid the $350 price tag of a genuine blank planchet by making his own (Chapter Eight), and decided to do a forgery of this coin, he could realize about a two or three hundred dollar profit for every single one he strikes.

The only problem is, every single one he strikes will have the exact same tiny scratch on Jefferson's cheek. If two of these forged nickels should ever cross paths (which happens) and their similarity is noticed (which also happens), they will be detected.[1] Published bulletins and photographs will then rapidly circulate through numismatic circles, and the forger will come to the conclusion that he'd be taking a great risk to ever attempt to market another one. People might even start remembering where they'd obtained the specimens he'd already sold.

To counteract this possibility, the forger can try a couple of things. He can make an effort to camouflage the genuine random contact marks on his forgeries by applying additional marks and "recirculating" them a bit to produce natural wear patterns, or he can attempt to remove the intaglio traces of the contact marks from his dies before striking his coins.

A true professional will probably even consider doing both.

This might seem surprising to a lot of people. Would a forger who went to all the trouble of transferring the exact image of an original coin onto a workable die really want to take a chance of ruining it by trying to touch it up by hand?

---

[1] Incredibly, this unlikely method is just about the *only* way some forgeries can ever be discovered!

Sure he would. Why not? The hardest part of engraving by hand is the layout and sinking of detail, and the die creation process the forger used has already accomplished this to perfection. Cleaning up and re-engraving small imperfections — or "dressing", as it is properly called — is a fairly straightforward, though admittedly time consuming procedure that doesn't require nearly as much expertise as engraving an entire die. What makes it even easier in this case is that all of the blemishes he wants to remove will have appeared on the coin as incuse scratches, nicks, and dings, and now appear on his dies as relief lines, lumps, and bumps. They can often be carefully worked out of the detail areas with little more than a fine tipped smooth burnishing tool, an Optivisor, and patience.[2] The field (being the highest part of the die) is even easier to dress, since it can be polished quite smooth and flat using nothing more than a piece of rouge emery cloth. Some forgers have become so adept at dressing dies that they can actually use a slightly worn coin (AU- 50/55) as a master and then "deepen" the fine detail in the die, successfully restoring what was lost, to enable them to strike coins in a much higher (and more valuable) grade than their original!

This sort of meticulous reworking is fairly uncommon, though. More often than not a forger will merely dress out the most obvious blemishes, smooth the field, and call the die good. The less noticeable marks are then confused and obscured by placing the struck forgery in a bag with other forgeries (or coins) and giving the bag a few good shakes. This will create a random series of minor blemishes on an otherwise uncirculated coin that most numismatists, for some strange reason, usually refer to as *bag marks*.[3]

Granted, a clean coin with an absence of bag marks is valued substantially higher than the more "average specimens" which have any number of them, but for that very reason it is also more likely to be subjected to the process of being professionally graded (and authenticated). If the forger doesn't relish the thought of having the impressions of his dies photographed and kept on file someplace to be periodically compared to similar coins as they are submitted, he will probably choose to generate just as much income in the long run by marketing "safer" grades of coins in greater volume.

---

[2] Just as with the hand engraving process described in Chapter Five, the forger will continually press small pieces of soft lead against his work as it progresses in order to check it.

[3] For coins in an uncirculated condition, gold coins (being softer than other alloys) tend to have far more bag marks than silver, copper, or nickel coins. Larger coins like half dollars and large cents are also more susceptible to bag marks than dimes, half dimes, small cents, and so forth. Careful forgers know this, and would not overdo the creation of bag marks on small coins.

Many of them will even be circulated — in fact, there is hardly anything *less* suspicious than a moderately circulated, evenly worn, convincingly toned, and otherwise generally unspectacular coin being offered for sale.

The pioneer forger Carl Wilhelm Becker was very much aware of this, since he would have probably had a difficult time explaining where he kept coming up with so many ancient coins that were still in mint condition! So he contrived to artificially "circulate" them by placing them in a covered bucket along with a handful of dirt and gravel, hanging the bucket from the axle of his buggy, and then "taking his coins for a little ride" out in the country, as he once put it.

After being bounced and jumbled around for 15 or 20 kilometers on the unpaved back roads of 18th century central Europe, Becker's forgeries were usually ready for the second stage of their treatment — applying a convincing patina (which we will get to in a moment).

While Becker's method worked admirably for him, unless a modern forger happens to be Amish, he isn't likely to do it quite the same way. A much more convenient (though less enjoyable) recipe for achieving similar results is to place about 2 cups of forgeries (or forgeries mixed with common coins) into a small lapidary rock tumbler, add 1 tablespoon of pea gravel, no more than 1/4 cup of very fine dirt (powdered, unfired

Lapidary rock tumbler ready to receive a standard "recipe" for creating wear, aging, and patina on two cups of forged ancient tetradrachms. A forger will want to make certain that the liquid seal on his drum is leakproof.

ceramic clay is perfect), a pinch of sulphur (optional), and around 3 cups of unrefined liquid uric acid (that's plain, old, ordinary pee, folks).

The forger then switches the tumbler on and allows it to slowly rotate overnight, for a week, for a month, or for however long it takes to achieve the desired level of "circulation" he is seeking to replicate.

As you've probably guessed by now, Becker's secret to producing a successful patina on his coins was the use of urine. He became something of an exotic expert in the area, claiming, for instance, that morning urine was better than afternoon urine; that a woman's urine turned bronze coins a different shade of green than a man's urine; or that the urine of a beer drinker produced different tones than that of a consumer of wine. Best results were usually obtained when the coins were also in contact with soil, and he found that different soils affected color and finish as well. His basic method was to bury a small cache of coins in a shallow hole and "sprinkle" the spot two or three times daily for a week or two, then recover them after about a month. Silver coins might have turned anything from gray to black, while bronze coins ranged from dark, chocolate brown to avocado green.

A successfully toned ancient coin — not overdone, and still retaining an appealing and presentable appearance, shown next to a freshly struck example of the same coin.

Modern forgers reproducing the effects and toning of ordinary, circulated coinage will seldom need to go beyond the tumbler method described above, but those who wish to imitate ancient coins, or other coins that have been buried, usually take a page from Becker's book and follow his method. It is still the best known.

Another feature of buried coinage — one that particularly applies to ancients, but which Becker didn't become too involved with — concerns the occasional presence of *pitting* on a coin's surface. This is especially common on bronze coinage, where sulphur in the air or soil has combined with moisture to form sulfuric acid, leaving corrosive specks and patches on a coin. At its worst, a pocket of corrosion can spread just below the coin's surface — creating a condition known as *bronze disease*.

The effect of advanced bronze disease, shown on the edge of a huge diobol of Ptolemy II. Here the subsurface corrosion has finally caused the coin's surface at the affected area to flake off, exposing a ragged core. While not particularly appealing, a small amount of bronze disease on an otherwise presentable specimen is generally tolerated by numismatists.

The forger can duplicate either effect by flicking or dabbing a small amount of battery acid onto the coin and letting it work prior to patinating the piece. Nothing further need be done afterward for a successful pitted effect, but to properly simulate a pocket of bronze disease the forger will next use a pin to scratch through the patina layer inside of a likely appearing pit, and then add a small amount of additional acid. When the surface of the coin within the pit forms a scummy fuzz he will not rinse it off, but simply leave it.[4] Either or both of these effects lend an incredibly persuasive impression of legitimacy to a forgery of an ancient bronze, but as they also affect market value, obviously a forger will want to avoid overdoing them.

There is one last category of aging that forgers often address, and that is the toning of uncirculated or nearly uncirculated pieces. Toning is basically a layer of light oxidation, in combination with other lightly reactive substances, deposited over time upon the mint luster of a new coin.

When a coin is actually struck by a pair of dies, its surface is distorted into a microscopic pattern of interlocking flow marks which, under

---

[4] This is the very way that bronze disease forms naturally. Sulfuric acid attacks bare bronze more readily than the protective layer of patina that has formed over the coin, so acid continuing to act within a pit will spread out to the bronze just beneath the surface, where it can become very difficult to treat or remove.

magnification, have a diamond-like shape to them. To the naked eye, this is the "frost" on the surface of an uncirculated coin, its mint luster.[5] When this surface changes color due to oxidation — but without experiencing actual wear — it is still a mint state surface. It is simply toned.

Toning is a very effective way for a forger to present uncirculated specimens of older coins, particularly copper issues. (While bright red large cents and Indian head cents do exist, they are uncommon enough to be considered remarkable.) He will use various methods, usually involving heat or light, to convert his freshly struck forgeries into beautifully toned "antiques".

One of the quickest and easiest ways is to simply lay the coin in a stainless steel spoon, and rest the spoon on top of an electric burner coil on a kitchen stove. As soon as the coin begins to "blush" (which only takes a minute or two) the spoon is removed and the coin allowed to cool. Another common technique is to place a coin in a paper envelope and expose it to low heat for a period of time. The different chemicals in various types of papers will give a variety of toning effects. (One of the most convincing ways to tone forgeries of early 20th century coinage is to wrap a stack of coins in a paper tube and place them in an oven. The toning will affect the edges of the pieces first and then leech gradually inward, exactly as it would if the coins had been stored somewhere for decades in paper coin rolls.) Simple ultraviolet light from direct sunlight will deepen the tone of a copper coin, even when it is sealed in plastic. Some plastics will tone coins, as will petroleum vapors. Forgers are an experimentive and resourceful lot, and will try and use anything that produces an effect that works.

And finally, I'll offer you the thought of what I can only describe as *reverse toning* — a forger's technique whereby he can actually restore a full, brilliant mint luster to an authentic coin that has somehow lost it, perhaps through cleaning. Not possible, you say? Well. . . think like a forger thinks, and recall that true mint luster can only be produced by striking. All he has to do is make up a custom set of electroplate nickel die shells, and *strike* the luster back on!

---

[5] For a forger to create true mint luster, his forgeries must be sharply struck, as with a minting machine, rather than slowly squeezed upon an arbor press.

Chapter Eleven

Detection and Protection

Several years ago, while participating on an archaeological dig sponsored by a local university, I assisted with the excavation of a stone pit house in the Book Cliffs region of the Colorado Plateau. Pot sherd patterns, stone tool designs, and style of construction gave our crew pretty solid evidence that we were dealing with a Fremont Indian culture dwelling, but we kept hoping to uncover something substantial enough to be considered proof. We finally found it about 30 centimeters down, under the lee of a collapsed stone wall.

The fire pit didn't look like much — it had no beauty or form that could be treasured as art — but we recognized its value at once, and considered it our most important discovery thus far.[1] Uncontaminated charcoal samples were painstakingly recovered, preserved, and sent to a laboratory where carbon-14 tests confirmed a date for our pit of approximately 1125 A.D., fixing it firmly within the Classic phase of the San Rafael Fremont variant.

Scientists have developed a remarkable variety of tools and methods for assigning reliable dates to material objects. At an undisturbed archaeological site, for example, *relative* chronology can be assigned to the deposition of artifacts based upon their superposition within clearly defined layers of occupation. *Absolute* dates for many materials — such as our fire pit charcoal — can then be established through sophisticated tests and accurate measurements: carbon-14, dendrochronology, obsidian hydration, archaeomagnetism, amino acid racemization, potassium argon radiometric decay, and thermoluminescence, to name but a few. Things like fireplace charcoal, seeds and pollen, textiles, pottery, skeletal remains, dinosaur bones, and even rocks can all be dated within reasonable parameters and with consistent results.

And yet — for all this — there is simply *no reliable test capable of determining the date of manufacture of a metal artifact.* A rusty, hand-wrought iron nail could be a relic of the True Cross or a part of the

---

[1] Real archaeology is not treasure hunting. Its value lies not in what you find, but in what you find out.

Mayflower or a souvenir from the blacksmith's forge at Colonial Williamsburg from last summer. We can guess all we please, but we simply have no way of knowing for sure.

In other words, if a forgery of a coin is properly done, there is really no reason it should ever be detected as a forgery by anyone.

But many forgeries, thankfully, have at least *something* about them that is not properly done, and so the matter of their detection becomes a sort of waiting game played between the forger, his victims, and those who attempt to authenticate numismatic items professionally.

The first coins to fall by the wayside will be those which fail to meet the nominal standards of size, weight, alloy, and types. Poor workmanship or inadequate manufacturing technique will expose still others, and of course there will always be some that are so unusual, or pristine, or just plain outlandish that they seem "too good to be true". For instance, a forger could easily create a brockage of an Indian head cent, but a brockage of an Indian head cent dated 1877 (the rarest year of issue) would be pushing it. A brockage of an Indian head cent dated 1877 on a clipped silver planchet intended for a dime that contains a lamination and was flipped out and struck a second time 30% off center — well, some forgers get so greedy they just don't know when to quit.

Most detection is much more difficult though, and some exceptionally well made forgeries may remain in the marketplace for years before being identified — if they ever are at all. One professional authenticator I know of once examined 114 examples of the 1916-S ten-dollar gold piece, gathered at random from different collections in widely scattered locations throughout the United States. *Sixty-four* of them turned out to be forgeries![2] That's 56% of the sample of just *one* type and date! This test was done around twenty years ago, and though pictures of this particularly excellent forgery have been published and circulated as a result, imagine how many forged 1916-S gold eagles were not discovered, and have since then changed hands as legitimate coins. Imagine also how many more have probably been introduced into numismatic circles. Do you own a 1916-S ten-dollar gold piece, by any chance?

Well, are you ready for more bad news?

---

[2] *Detecting Counterfeit Gold Coins*, Book 2, by John Devine, Heigh Ho Printing Co, Newbury Park, California, 1977.

The 1916-S gold eagle is hardly in a class by itself. For quite some time now it has been an accepted fact that virtually *all* U.S. gold issues have been extensively forged — the common dates right along with the more scarce ones. From about 1870 on, in fact, there is hardly a single year that forgeries haven't been discovered for — and this accounts for just the ones that actually *have* been discovered. Certainly no one can make the claim that all forgery types in this series that have ever been produced have been or even can be identified. These gold coins are particularly popular with forgers for a number of reasons, chief of which is that they are so easy to strike and work with compared to any other alloy. That, along with the guarantee of a comfortable premium over their bullion value for even common date coins in reasonable (if not choice) condition, has made gold coins the most commonly forged of all numismatic items.

But who is doing all of this forgery, anyway? Our 2,800 potential forgers we targeted way back in Chapter One?

Yes — and no. Partly, at any rate. The purpose of this book has been to describe the practical principles, methods, and techniques employed in the private manufacture of rare coins by larcenous-minded individuals, people who work alone and possess modest skill and resources, but lack access to the sort of highly sophisticated, expensive, or exotic equipment that is difficult for the normal person to obtain. But there is another type of numismatic forger that we haven't focused on here yet who does not work alone, who has considerable resources and financial backing, and who can readily obtain the latest, state-of-the-art equipment in whatever form is needed. I am speaking, of course, of private minting operations conducted by foreign crime syndicates.

Ever since the early 1950s, when counterfeit U.S. gold pieces began flowing out of Hong Kong, numismatic forgery has been used by organized crime in various locations as a convenient means of disposing of bullion and reaping additional profits while converting gold into cash. Then, with the sharp rise in price of bullion beginning in the 1970s, and the correspondingly greater increase in the numismatic value of coins, full-blown forgery for profit became an end in itself. Cast coins were supplanted by die-struck pieces, and much greater attention began to be given to standards and quality. Some of the processes described in this book are known to have been used for much of this foreign die making — primarily casting and explosive impact copying — but the sheer volume of output such operations were capable of made it more or less inevitable that the "four practical ways for forgers to create dies" described earlier in this book would be augmented by a fifth method involving a modern, highly specialized non-traditional machining process known as EDM (Electrical Discharge Machining).

The technology used in the EDM process had its beginnings back in the 1940s, with the development of carbon-arc metal disintegrators designed for removing broken off taps and drill bits from blind holes in metal. On these simpler machines, a vibrating engraver drives a carbon electrode into the work as an electric spark eats the metal away, leaving behind a clean hole. EDM machines are the ultra-sophisticated, exotic cousins of the metal disintegrator, capable of three-dimensional relief milling with exquisite detail and fineness.[3] They are often used in commercial applications for die making — utilizing ultrasonically machined graphite electrodes produced from full-sized master models — which of course makes them ideally suited for use in numismatic forgery, as well. I'm not going to go into a lot of detail here about how they operate, though, since the $25,000-$50,000 price tag on them is enough to keep most private forgers from rushing right out and hauling one home to stick in his garage or basement. It is enough for us to know that the large-scale foreign forging operations have ready access to this sort of equipment via the free world market. In recent years, most gold forgeries using EDM technology have been originating in the Middle East, primarily from Lebanon.

But while EDM can do an excellent job of appropriating the images from authentic coins in order to create superior dies for forgery, the only advantage it holds over the methods described in this book is its greater adaptability to higher production levels. Plating, hubbing, explosive impact copying, and even casting can do the job just as well on a smaller scale, and will produce struck forgeries of equally superior quality.

Which brings us right back to our larcenous-minded individual forger — who is apt to forge not only gold, but anything else he has an inkling or an opportunity to do. What all of us would like to know is how to be able to detect his forgeries.

Unfortunately, I can't tell you. There are no hard and fast rules, no magic formulas. Detection of poor quality forgeries isn't too difficult to learn,

---

[3] I am told that Japan and Switzerland are currently the world leaders in the development and production of EDM technology, though several other countries (including the United States) are also involved.

but if a layman encounters enough of them and nothing else, he can easily become lulled into the mindset that all forgeries should be just as obvious — which is simply not the case. I agree that there ought to be a better way for a collector to be able to authenticate a heavily patinated ancient coin on the spot other than popping it in his mouth to see if it tastes like urine (no, I am not recommending this), but I don't know what it could be. Other than accumulated knowledge, experience, a detailed visual examination under magnification, and a comparison of measurable standards, there is really little else the average person has to go on. With some forgeries this will sometimes be enough, and for others it never will be.

So while I may not be able to provide many useful clues for detection, I hope I can at least offer a few suggestions that may give some degree of better protection.

First: **There needs to be a greater awareness among numismatists regarding our vulnerability to forgery.**

I've always been a believer in the old adage that "to be forewarned is to be forearmed", and I hope you are, too. After all, if you can discover a good reason why you should be more cautious, you may better determine how to use more caution. Perhaps it would be an oversimplification to suggest that the exposure of Becker's coins as forgeries in the early 19th century was the primary cause leading to the eventual cataloging and classifying of genuine ancient die varieties, but there can be no doubt that it did have some impact. Similarly, the discovery in the 1960s that the obverse image on a number of gold dollars dated 1862 was struck with the very same die[4] used for other coins dated 1874 and 1887, revealed all three to be false — providing authenticators with one obverse and three reverse die varieties that, as known forgeries, can be checked against other coins bearing those dates. In each of these cases, information was compiled and precautions developed only after a clear need was realized.

Reading this book will have been an excellent way to begin to shatter many of the commonly held myths and misconceptions about the supposed difficulty of numismatic forgery. By endeavoring to take you, the reader, by the hand and leading you step-by-step through a "hands on" experience, my hope has been to help dispel the false sense of security that has existed among so many coin collectors, dealers, and investors for far too long.

---

[4] Each and every die — even among modern, mass-produced dies — bears tiny "fingerprints" of individuality that can often be differentiated if enough study is done. The forgeries mentioned above have led to the discovery and cataloging of 53 separate obverse dies and 47 reverse dies used to mint authentic 1862 gold dollars.

Armed with this radically new information and a keener awareness, you should be in a much better position to learn ways to protect yourself.

Which raises a thoughtful question: If you feel that you've found this material to be interesting and useful, wouldn't it be a considerate act on your part to purchase an additional copy of this book as a gift for a fellow numismatist? Or while you're at it, why not (ahem,) purchase two more copies?

*Second: **Acquire numismatic items only from persons you know and can trust, and who offer a guarantee of authenticity.***

Or as your mother once taught you, don't accept candy from strangers. This is a sensible enough rule to follow in any case, but the increasing prospect of getting stuck with an excellent quality forgery makes it all the more relevant. Most numismatic dealers are honest, of course, but there will always be a few (recall our demonstration of one percent of any group possessing larcenous intent?) who may not be above passing along a forged coin that they themselves had lost money on. And then again, while many dealers are quite good at detecting the more obvious forgeries they come across, we must remember that dealers simply are not authenticators, and that forgeries do occasionally get by the best of them. When a dealer purchases a forgery thinking it's an authentic coin, he'll sooner or later end up selling it as an authentic coin.

It's also a good idea not to purchase anything you are completely unfamiliar with until you've either had a chance to study enough about it to learn what to look for, or unless you feel certain you can trust the seller. This is sometimes asking a lot, though. Coin collectors (and to a certain degree, investors also) are frequently drawn into new areas and fields as their eclectic interests range freely about. One person may have spent years collecting nothing else but U.S. type coins of the 19th and 20th centuries, for instance, but after reading a book about the Punic Wars or watching the film *Sparticus* on HBO, he may develop an overpowering urge to own a Roman coin. Another person may have accumulated an impressive portfolio of choice uncirculated Morgan silver dollars, but then receive a favorable tip about the investment potential of Canadian gold proofs. Either of these buyers are likely to make a purchase at the first available opportunity, which may or may not be from someone that they happen to be familiar with.

Coin *dealers* are more vulnerable than anyone, though, since a large portion of their acquisitions may routinely come from people they don't know, have never seen before, and will likely never see again. Any thought of obtaining a "guarantee" under such circumstances can only be so much wishful thinking.

Under these circumstances, my recommendation is to *never pay cash* for coins purchased from walk-ins off the street. Ever. *Always* issue a check, so that you will at least have a name to go with a purchase — and try to obtain an address as well from some form of identification, "for your records". True, a forger can easily use a false name, but he will also need a false ID to cash his check. And while he can do this too, it won't take long before it becomes inconvenient and expensive to keep up with all the paperwork necessary to keep track of a number of different identities. At the very least it can provide one more obstacle to the forger, and anything that serves to make a forger less anonymous is helpful.

And whether you are a collector, an investor, a dealer, or just a tourist, *never* purchase gold coins overseas, no matter how attractive the deal being offered may seem, unless you are paying close to bullion prices for them. In all likelihood, all you will end up with is bullion.

Third: **Train yourself to anticipate and look for forgeries.**

Few significant discoveries were made by stumbling upon something by accident; most were the result of a long, intentional, deliberate search. (Even Columbus was looking for *something* when he found America — even though it was something else.)

After reading this book you should at the very least be thinking a great deal more about forgery, and a little healthy suspicion can, in this case, be a very positive habit to cultivate. Ideally, a numismatist should make the issue of possible forgery a part of the routine examination of every coin he handles. But in order to do this properly, he will need access to better information and better tools than he normally has at present. In other words, he should have resources at least as good as those a forger will use.

Information should be the easiest thing to obtain, particularly regarding accurate, measurable standards, but this isn't always the case. If a good forger is going to make an error on something like his collar diameter, for example, he's only going to be off a *little* bit. It will probably too little to see, a person could reason, but not too little to measure. So. . . we pull out our trusty machinist's 6" calipers (Chapter Two) and open up our latest copy of the *Red Book* — and what does it tell us? Amid other interesting information about standards, the diameter of a Coronet type gold quarter eagle is listed as "18mm". A three dollar gold piece is "20.5mm", and a five dollar coin is recorded as having a diameter of "21.6mm".

What's wrong with this, you ask? Only the fact that the most readily measurable characteristic of a coin's standards — its diameter — is typically given to an accuracy of only a tenth of a millimeter! This is simply too coarse a measuring standard: if we had nothing but this record to go by, we couldn't even detect the margin of error most forgeries would fall within.

I would love to see the *Red Book* (which is probably one of the most widely relied upon numismatic sources in use), as well as other reference works, pick up one more decimal place and list all diameter measurements for machine-struck, collar formed, modern coinage in *hundredths* of a millimeter. This practice really should become standard. Then we would know that our quarter eagle should actually measure 17.94mm,[5] the three dollar piece is accurate at 20.50mm, and our half eagle had better be 21.56mm, or we're in trouble. Even with allowances made for manufacturing variances such as collar erosion, I know that I would feel safer knowing that the true diameter of a Buffalo nickel should be exactly 21.17mm, rather than simply "something close to 21.2mm", wouldn't you?

Which brings us to the matter of measuring tools. . . A decent pair of machinist's 6" calipers will measure accurately to a hundredth of a millimeter, but for a number of reasons it isn't the best of things to use on coins. Unless they are handled very delicately, the precision ground stainless steel jaws can crush, mar, flatten, or otherwise deform edge reeding and detail, particularly on soft gold coins. (I don't know of a single dealer in his right mind who would be willing to allow a perfect stranger to take a pair of steel calipers to one of his coins.) Cheap plastic calipers, on the other hand, aren't accurate enough to detect the tolerances necessary to detect forgeries. Machinist's 6" calipers are also too bulky to be conveniently portable. They are delicate instruments and must be carried about in a case, which also adds to their bulk.

---

[5] At these fine tolerances, even slight circulation wear will affect measurements, especially on coins with reeded edges. Still, the listing of maximum and minimum variances (+ or - so-and-so) could aid greatly in exposing some (but not all) forgeries. (Incidentally, any Coronet type gold quarter eagle that measures 18.00mm is too large in diameter to be a genuine mint issue. It would have to be a forgery.)

If I were going to redesign a pair of machinist's calipers specifically for use by numismatists, the first thing I'd do is make them smaller by reducing the measuring capacity from 6" to 2". (How many 6" coins do you come across, anyway?) I'd eliminate the hole depth measuring probe on the end opposite the jaws, since it is unnecessary, and likewise do away with the small pair of inside measuring jaws on top. I'd line the measuring planes of the jaws with replaceable shims made of some substance like nylon, which would remain firm but do no damage to coins, and I'd retain the battery powered digital readout meter with its on/off switch, automatic zero reset, and inches to metric conversion button.

I haven't come across anything like this, but I'd like to. If any company that markets numismatic products would care to come out with one, please package it in a cushioned, snap-shut holder that will fit in a pocket, and include a reference table listing precise diameters and wear variances for a wide assortment of popular coins.

Lacking an adequate measuring device in the meantime, a 10-power magnifying lens or a 16-power jewelers loupe remains the most useful tool available for inspecting coins. Many otherwise excellent forgeries will, under magnification, reveal traces of carelessness on the forger's part that are not noticeable to the naked eye — minute blemishes from the surface of a cast die, random EDM "spikes", dressing or polishing marks, and so forth. The American Numismatic Association periodically issues bulletins and updates describing such features on recently discovered forgeries, which I'd like to see reprinted in leading coin magazines on a regular basis.

Fourth: **Use authentication services.**

Originally conceived as certification agencies to assign strict grading classifications to individual coins, authentication services have more and more taken on the responsibility of determining whether numismatic items are genuine or not. Once received, coins are submitted to a variety of non-destructive tests that are normally too elaborate or impractical for the average person to perform, such as accurate specific gravity determination or X-ray spectrography. They are closely examined under high magnification, photographed, and compared with known genuine examples as well as any known forgeries of each particular specimen.

These agencies maintain extensive files and cross references, registering each coin they certify as well as recording each forgery they detect. In addition to authentication, grading, and registering, many services also offer *encapsulation* — or "slabbing", as it is sometimes called — where coins are sonically sealed in protective, tamper-proof cases in order to preserve their condition and guarantee their legitimacy.

Authentication services provide the highest level of protection and assurance to the numismatist that he can get, but while the cost can be considered reasonable, it is not necessarily cheap. It makes a great deal of sense to have any extremely valuable coin authenticated, as well as any coin suspected of being a forgery, but the process often adds too much expense to the cost of trading coins of more modest value (— a point which forgers are fully aware of, by the way). Generally, each numismatist will need to decide whether authentication services or encapsulation are practical for any particular coin. As a collector and a historian, I like to occasionally "handle" my coins (although gently), so while I have had some coins authenticated, I personally prefer to acquire slightly circulated examples that do not need to be encapsulated. Excessively rare coins, patterns, or specimens in pristine condition should be protected, however, and encapsulation provides an excellent way of doing so.

The use of authentication services with encapsulation is especially appropriate for the numismatic investor, who most often deals with coins of high value in exceptional condition. He will find that slabbed coins are far more liquid in the marketplace than loose coins, as their authenticity and precise grade are regarded as established value factors. Frankly, I don't see why any serious investor would want to consider acquiring anything other than authenticated, encapsulated coins.

I do have a couple of recommendations to make about them, however. For one thing, the date of encapsulation should appear on the slab. As technological developments progress or interpretations of grading standards shift (as happens), knowing when a particular coin was sealed could someday prove very helpful. I'd also like to suggest that agencies implement a "re-encapsulation" service. For a modest fee, slabbed coins could be opened, inspected and compared with previously registered data, and re-sealed in the most recently developed, up-to-date style of slab. One possibility would be to offer this service automatically whenever an encapsulated coin is sold or changes hands, registering the name of the new owner in the coin's file.

Fifth: **Prevent known forgeries from ever being mistaken for legitimate coins**

If you submit a coin to an expert for authentication and your worst suspicions are confirmed — you have a forgery — for heaven's sake *don't pass it on to anyone else.* Either mark it or destroy it, and write the loss off on your taxes.

The above measures should help, and will certainly provide better protection to the numismatist against forgery than remaining in the dark or taking no action at all, but they aren't meant as a guarantee. Even the best protection possible cannot be absolute. Anything that can be created by one human being sooner or later can be recreated by another human being. Perfect forgeries are not only perfectly possible, they already exist.

So suppose the worst actually happens. Suppose a forgery not only gets by your dealer, but comes back to you from a prestigious authentication service as a registered, encapsulated, genuine specimen. What then?

Well, I guess I'd have to say that Mark Hofmann probably put it best when he said, "If I can produce something so correctly, *so perfect* that the experts declare it to be genuine, then for all practical purposes it *is* genuine." You may as well own it, and value it, and esteem it, and regard it as an authentic item. You will be deceived, but no more so than everyone else.

And I'm sure Mr. Hofmann would agree, but if you want to ask him you will have to visit him in prison.

View of the forgery of the 1914-D cent from Chapter Three, showing the reverse of the same coin planed smooth and clearly marked as a forgery. This coin will never be able to mislead anyone as to its true nature.

APPENDIX

Heat Treating of Metals

The following material is intended to represent information which is readily available through a wide variety of sources, and would normally be obtained and used by a numismatic forger during the course of his activities.

Ferrous Metals

Annealing

By definition, annealing is the process whereby steel is softened (made more malleable) by heating it to a high temperature and allowing it to cool slowly. Generally steel is annealed to render it soft enough for machining or tooling, and to reduce internal strains in the metal caused by forging prior to hardening and tempering.

Temperatures for the most effective annealing depend upon the type of steel being treated, and should be slightly above the metal's "critical points" — or the temperatures at which internal changes take place within its structure.[1] For low carbon steel an annealing temperature of 1650°F works well; high carbon steel 1400° to 1500°; and high speed steel 1400°. Most annealing, though, is simply done by bringing the metal to a "low red heat", and the longer the cooling time, the softer the metal will be.

Hardening

Hardening may be described as the process of raising the temperature of steel up to its decalescence point and then quenching it in a suitable cooling medium. In practice, the "low red heat" point is perfectly suitable.

Quenching has the effect of permanently fixing the structural change in the metal which occurs when it reached the decalescence point, causing

---

[1] The two critical points are known as the *decalescence* point, which occurs when the temperature of the metal is rising, and the *recalescence* point, which is reached when the temperature is falling. For most practical purposes, the difference between them (about 20°F) is usually too slight to be concerned with.

the metal to remain hard. Cold brine (salt water) as a quench will produce a very hard effect on steel, while warm oil will harden it "softer".

Hardened steel has virtually no ductility or malleability at all, and is almost as brittle as glass. In order to be able to place any amount of stress (work force) on it, it must be tempered.

Tempering

Tempering is the process of reheating previously hardened steel to a low heat point and then allowing it to cool or quenching it, in order to toughen the metal and make it less brittle. Proper tempering requires practice and skill, since the process not only makes hardened steel less brittle, but also slightly softens it. The toughness and softness obtained in tempering depends upon the temperature to which the metal is raised; the more heat applied the less brittle, but also the less hard.

The level of heat applied to steel during tempering is often based upon a color temperature scale. Heated steel acquires a very thin film of oxidation which grows thicker and changes color as the temperature rises. All effective tempering levels occur within this color range.

Color	Temperature in °F
Very pale yellow	430°
Light yellow	440°
Pale straw-yellow	450°
Straw-yellow	460°
Deep straw-yellow	470°
Dark yellow	480°
Yellow-brown	490°
Brown-yellow	500°
Spotted red-brown	510°

Brown-purple	520°
Light purple	530°
Full purple	540°
Dark purple	550°
Full blue	560°
Dark Blue	570°
Very dark blue	600°

Case Hardening

This is a process in which a hard skin is applied to a localized portion of a piece of steel by heating and "soaking" the metal in a carboniferous compound. Steels which are case hardened exhibit tool-steel toughness at their working surfaces, while remaining more resilient at their cores. Case hardening is ideally suited to tools which must maintain their form while being subjected to shock stress, such as punches, dies, and so forth.

The portion of the work to be case hardened is heated to the decalescence point (low red) and then dipped in a commercially available *hardening powder*, which will melt and adhere to the metal — the longer the heat is applied, the thicker the case skin will develop. After sufficient heating time the metal is quenched to harden it, and then tempered.

Non-Ferrous Metals

Heat treating of non-ferrous metals and alloys is essentially a process of annealing, since hardening occurs as compression stress is applied during working and forming.

Silver and silver alloys

The ideal temperature for annealing silver is 1200°F, at which point the crystalline structure of the metal reaches its most malleable arrangement.

(A visible indication of this temperature is a deep pink internal glow.) This structure is then "fixed" in a way that is the exact opposite of that used for ferrous metals — it is cooled rapidly by quenching. As a rule, the quicker it is cooled, the softer the metal will be. Close attention must be paid to temperature, since heating silver past 1200°F will not increase the annealing effect, but will damage the integrity of the crystal lattice.

Copper and copper alloys

Copper is annealed in exactly the same manner as silver. In order to prevent the formation of firescale as the metal is heated, the metal may be coated with Handy and Harmon cream flux (or a similar silver soldering flux). This flux will turn liquid and glassy at about 1100°F which will indicate that the correct annealing temperature has nearly been reached. Quenching in a pickling solution will remove the flux easily.

Gold and gold alloys

Although pure gold does not become appreciably less ductile by working it, annealing can assist it to become slightly more malleable so that less force is required to form it from one shape to another. Gold alloys, however, will become significantly work hardened due to the compression of the other metals in solution with the gold, and may also be softened by annealing.

High gold alloys (18k and above) are usually annealed simply by heating the metal to a low red glow and allowing it to air cool. Medium to low gold alloys (16k and lower) may be annealed the same as for silver and copper, with heating followed by a quench.

GLOSSARY

Aging

The process of producing an artificial pattern of wear and/or toning to a forgery in order to make it appear old, used, and genuine.

Alloy

The composition or blend of various metals and their proportion that is used for any particular coin.

Alteration (altered coin)

A legitimate coin that has been illegally modified in order to make it appear to be a completely different (and more valuable) coin.

Ancient Coinage

Term covering the coins produced and coinage processes used from the beginnings of true coins (circa 7th century B.C.) up to and including the Byzantine period (about 1000 A.D.). Generally, ancient coinage was hammer-struck on thick, often irregular planchets.

Annealing

The process of making a piece of metal softer by proper treatment with heat. The opposite of hardening.

Authentication Service

Any of several private agencies which will, for a fee, examine coins submitted to them in order to determine whether the coins are authentic or not. In addition to type and detail study, a coin is usually subjected to a series of accurate and sophisticated examinations of its physical properties.

Bag Marks

The slight nicks, scratches, and bruises that appear on the surface of almost all otherwise uncirculated coins as a result of coming into contact with other coins shortly after manufacture. To simulate, a forgery is placed in a bag with coins or other forgeries and shaken.

Banker's Marks

Small, geometric-shaped counterstamps applied to the surfaces of ancient coins by various money changers as an indication that they had examined a particular coin and determined it to be genuine. Unless unusually rare, attractive, and well placed, banker's marks tend to slightly lower the value of an ancient coin to a collector — but for that very reason they add a nice touch of authenticity to a forgery. *See also Test Cut.*

Blank (blanking)

The term blank refers to a disc of alloy sheared from a sheet by a punch and die in a process known as blanking. A blank that is to be struck inside of a collar is referred to as a planchet only after it receives its upset edge; a blank that is to be broadstruck without a collar becomes a planchet only after it receives an ornamented edge applied by edge marking machinery, unless no edge marking was originally used on the coin, in which case the blank can be considered a finished planchet. Confused? Go have a beer and don't think about it for a while, or see *Broadstruck, Collar, Ornamented Edge, Planchet, and Upset Edge.*

Broadstruck

Term for a coin which has been compressed between an upper and a lower die, with nothing present to restrain the flow of the planchet's metal from around the edges of the dies. A variation in striking pressure will result in coins of slightly different diameter, even if the planchets were identical to begin with. All coins were broadstruck prior to the development of the collar. *See Collar.*

Brockage

A mint error produced by a freshly minted coin serving as a "die" to one surface of a new, soft planchet as it is being struck. The first coin produces an intaglio image of its contact surface upon the planchet, creating a brockage. The brockage principle can be used to create satisfactory dies for limited use in forgery. *See Stress Hardened.*

Bronze Disease

The chemical degeneration of the bronze alloy of ancient coins, resulting in irregular surface pitting. Not all ancient bronzes exhibit the symptoms of bronze disease, but when successfully imitated on a forgery it can be a convincingly deceptive indication of true antiquity. *See Pitting.*

Bullion

Processed, precious metal sold to the public, usually in the form of bars or ingots. Silver is almost always sold pure (.999 fine), while gold may be alloyed (as with the Krugerrand) or offered pure (as in the Maple Leaf).

Cabinet Friction

Older coins that have been part of collections in the past were often stored flat on trays in cabinets, and as a result usually bear evidence of slight scuffing or faint scratches upon their highest areas of relief. Should not be overlooked as a convincing way to help substitute for the lack of a documented provenience for a forgery of a rare coin in exceptional condition.

Case Hardening

The heat treating of mild steel by adding carbon to the surface only of an object, producing a tool that is hard at its work surface while remaining resilient at its core. *See Hardening Powder.*

Casting

The creating of an object by introducing molten metal into a mold. *See Lost Wax Process.*

Centrifuge

A spring-driven, rotating arm which creates centrifugal force in order to force molten metal into a mold under great pressure, resulting in superior, intricate detail in the object being cast.

Clipped Planchet

Refers to a minting error caused by striking a coin upon an imperfect planchet with a crescent-shaped portion missing from the edge. Difficult to forge by altering a normal coin, but simple to forge by striking from dies.

Collar

A circular restraining ring which encases a planchet while being struck by upper and lower dies, assuring a perfectly round coin of consistent size. In effect, a collar constitutes a "third die", and is used in the manufacture of all modern coinage. There are three forms of collars: plain, reeded, and segmented.

Counterfeit

An unauthorized, illegally produced duplicate of an officially issued coin, created with the express intent of using it for the same purpose as the genuine coin was designed to be used.

Denticles

The elongated, tooth-shaped border elements found around the edges of most broadstruck coins minted between about 1650 to 1850. Denticles produced a wide, satisfactory edge for coins struck by a screw press; but when collars came into widespread use, a finer edge was possible and denticles became unnecessary. *See Rim.*

Device

Any major element incorporated into a coin's design, such as a portrait, allegorical figure, heraldic device, etc.

Diamonds

The effect, under magnification, of the "frost" on the surface of an uncirculated coin. It is impossible to create this effect chemically or by cleaning. It can be produced only by striking.

Die

One of a pair of tools bearing the intaglio image of a coin, which are pressed at great pressure into a blank planchet, producing a coin. *See Pile and Trussel.*

Die Axis

The orientation of a coin's reverse side to its obverse side, usually expressed in terms of the hour hand of a clock. In a coin with a die axis of 12:o'clock, the top of the reverse would meet the coin's rim at the same point as the top of the obverse; at 6:o'clock the bottom of the reverse would meet the rim at the same point as the top of the obverse, and so forth. (Note:The terms coin axis and medallion axis are sometimes used to refer to coins with die orientations of 6:o'clock and 12:o'clock, respectively.)

Die Variety

When dies for coinage were produced largely by hand, subtle differences inevitably occurred whenever two or more dies were created for the same style of coin. A date may be larger or smaller, a star placed differently, or the main device moved closer to the rim, for instance. Only the complete mechanization of die production in modern times has reduced this, but occasionally die varieties within a coinage series may still occur.

Differential Shrinkage

In metal casting, the end product will actually be slightly smaller than the mold into which the molten metal was introduced due to the mass of the hot liquid shrinking somewhat as it solidifies and cools. This difference is ordinarily compensated for by creating a mold slightly larger than the finished cast.

Ductile

The quality of a metal which allows it to be elongated by drawing, hammering, or rolling without severely stressing or cracking the metal in the process. Pure gold is extremely ductile; hardened steel is not, but is usually made more ductile by tempering or annealing. The opposite of brittle. *See Malleable.*

Edge Marking (and lettering)

A pattern of designs or writing upon the outside edge of a coin. It may appear as either incuse or relief, and be applied by a collar, before striking within a collar, or without the involvement of a collar at all. This term is not usually used to describe a reeded edge. *See Ornamented edge; Reeded Edge.*

Electroplating

Process by which an object is coated with a thin layer of metal, deposited by the passing of an electrical current through a solution to the object being plated. Fully plated base metal forgeries are not effective in that they are easily detectable, yet it is possible to expertly alter coins using this method, as well as to create serviceable coin dies.

Engraving (of dies)

The creating of coin dies by artistically removing from a die blank that metal which will leave an intaglio impression of the coin to be produced. This procedure requires great skill and practice to achieve satisfactory results, and even under the best of circumstances minor variations from the original coin being copied will occur. For this reason, die engraving is more suitable for creating copies of ancient and medieval coinage than for modern coins.

Error

A coin which has left the mint containing a noticeable manufacturing defect. The forging of errors is a relatively simple way to turn common coins into preferred collector items. *See Brockage; Mule; Multiple Strike Error; Off Center; Off Metal.*

Explosive Impact Copying

The creating of dies for forgery by driving the image of a genuine coin into a steel blank with explosive force, causing the steel to take the image of the coin so quickly that the softer coin literally does not have "time" to spread out or flatten. Some of the best forgeries known have been produced using this method, and the best of these are virtually undetectable.

Fabric

The sensory quality of a coin that gives one the impression of its legitimacy. Factors such as look, feel, heft, and tone — as well as style, evidence of method of manufacture, and wear patterns, all combine to make a coin "seem" right. A forgery must successfully imitate the fabric of a genuine coin to be deceptive.

Fantasy

A coin which represents no type which ever actually existed, such as a mule of a 1959 Lincoln cent obverse with a wheat cent reverse, or an ancient pattern that is the invention of a forger's whim. Frequently an unwise or overconfident forger will attempt to create an "ultra-rarity" — only to produce a laughable fantasy.

Field

The flat background of a coin, upon which rise in relief such elements as devices, legends, denticles or rims, etc. On a die, the field is the highest surface, and may easily be polished to a fine, smooth finish.

Forgery

An unauthorized, illegally produced duplicate of an officially issued coin, created with the express intent of deceiving the collector's market into accepting it as a genuine item.

Gravity Hammer

A mechanical improvement over hand-hammered coinage, in which a heavy weight is dropped down a controlled guide to strike the upper die. Gravity hammers are slow but capable of producing enormous force, and were in common use during the 16th century by the central European Germanic states to mint large, multiple units of the silver thaler. Because of its simplicity of construction and ease of control over the force produced, the gravity hammer is especially suitable for use by the forger.

Hammered Coinage

Term which effectively describes the method of manufacture of nearly all Western coinage during the first 2,000 years of its existence. A blank planchet, placed upon a lower die, is covered with an upper die which is then struck with a hammer from one to several times. Generally replaced during the 17th century by mechanical devices.

Hardening

Treatment of metal, usually by heat, to transform its crystalline structure so as to make it less ductile and malleable. *See also Stress Hardened, Tempering.*

Hardening Powder

Any of several commercially available carboniferous compounds which, when applied to red-hot steel and allowed to "soak in" for any length of time at about 2000° Fahrenheit, will produce a case hardened skin on the surface of the metal.

Hoard

A contemporary group of coins that were lost, hidden, or otherwise abandoned at some time in the past, and rediscovered later. Often a number of forgeries can be marketed at one time if represented as part of a newly discovered hoard.

Hot Striking

Many large ancient coins were struck on such thick cast planchets that not enough force could be produced during hammer striking to bring up the detail on the dies. Also, dies were softer than modern dies, being made usually of bronze. The solution was to heat the planchets prior to striking, making them far more malleable. After minting, hot struck coins were quickly pickled to remove scale. *See Malleable, Pickling.*

Hub

A full size, positive image in hardened steel of either the major elements of a coin face, or the complete image of the coin. Used to press into a soft die blank to produce dies. The brockage principle can be used by the forger in exactly the same way. *See Brockage.*

Incuse

Detail in a positive image that is below the surface of the surrounding area. On a Morgan silver dollar, the word LIBERTY on the coronet in Liberty's hair is incuse. The opposite of relief.

Intaglio

An image that is usually incuse and always mirror image of the original, as on a coin die. The opposite of positive.

Intent

The motivation for counterfeiting or forgery is to make an illegal profit; the intent in doing so is to defraud someone by representing the false article as authentic. A touchy legal point, intent need not necessarily be demonstrated (by attempting to sell a forgery), but may well be presumed (by having merely produced a forgery).

Investment Plaster

A special type of very fine-grained plaster (*not* common Plaster of Paris!) used for investing wax images to create molds for casting using the lost wax process.

Lamination

A fold or imperfectly bonded layer of metal on a portion of the surface of a coin, caused by an impurity in the planchet prior to striking. Ancient coinage (especially bronze and brass) was highly susceptible to laminations, due to imperfect alloying methods.

Legend

The information pertaining to a coin's value, denomination, place of origin, issuing authority, and so forth that is usually found on either or both sides of a coin around the inside edge of its rim or border.

Lost Wax Process

A method of creating molds for casting by investing plaster around a wax model of the object to be cast. When the plaster sets, the mold is turned upside-down and heated, causing the wax to melt and burn out, thus becoming "lost". The resulting mold will contain detail of very high quality. *See also Centrifuge; Investment Plaster; Sprue.*

Machine-Struck Coinage

Also sometimes referred to as milled coinage, coins which have been struck by any of several mechanical means, at first without and later with the aid of a collar, starting around the middle of the 16th century. Followed hammered coinage.

Malleable

The property of a metal which enables it to be formed, or pressed, into another shape. A metal which has been annealed is usually ductile enough to be malleable. High heat will make even the least ductile metals temporarily malleable, until they cool.

Medieval Coinage

Hammer-struck coinage produced during the four centuries after the Byzantine period, prior to the Renaissance. Coins were normally broad, flat, and thin, with poor artistry and very shallow detail. Design elements and lettering on dies were usually made up using a series of small, standard shaped punches, while planchets were cut by snips or chisels from hammered sheet metal. The large number of uncataloged die varieties, the crudity with which dies were made, and the simplicity of manufacture all combine to make medieval coinage particularly vulnerable to modern forgery.

Mint

An officially sanctioned workplace where legitimate coins are manufactured. The making of coins by a mint is called minting, their product mint issues.

Mint Luster

Prior to striking, blank planchets are normally annealed, cleaned (pickled), and tumbled, producing a very bright, even finish. Coins struck from such planchets will likewise be clean and shiny. *See also Diamonds; Toning.*

Modern Coinage

In essence, all coins that are machine-struck with a collar, from dies produced by a master hub, are considered to be modern coinage. Since types are well standardized, dies for forgery are created using images from actual coins.

Mule

A coin produced using the obverse die from one coin and the reverse die from another. This sometimes — but very rarely — occurred during brief periods of transition from one coinage type to another, but more often than not any previously "undiscovered" mules appearing today are fantasies produced by forgers.

Multiple Strike Error

A coin or planchet that has been struck by dies, usually off-center, more than one time. An error highly prized by collectors that rarely escapes from the mint, multiple strike errors can easily be fashioned by the forger using good quality homemade dies. *See Off Center.*

Noncirculating Legal Tender

"Coins" struck by the authority of a government, bearing a denomination of monetary worth, but which are never intended to circulate as money. An example would be the current series of Saint-Gaudens style U.S. gold, the intrinsic value of which is ridiculously out of proportion to its stated value. Such coins are actually ingots, and are made expressly for sale to collectors and investors. Technically speaking, the forging of such items would actually be counterfeiting, not forgery.

Numismatic

The scientific field of interest having to do with various forms of money — particularly coins.

Obverse

The "front" side of a coin, bearing the primary device regarded as most significant by the authority issuing the coin. With dies, the obverse is the lower die for hammer-struck coins, the upper for modern.

Off Center

A planchet that has been only partially struck by dies, leaving part of the coin blank. Also a regular coin that has been struck again in such a manner. *See Error; Multiple Strike Error.*

Off Metal

A coin that has been struck on a planchet intended for a different coin. Examples would be a cent struck on a dime planchet, a nickel struck on a cent planchet, a half dollar struck on a quarter planchet, etc. — all of which are extremely practicable for a forger possessing good dies. The most famous off metal coin is probably the 1943 bronze cent. *See Error.*

Ornamented Edge

An elaborate and decorative edge, usually in relief, applied to coins by a separate, edge marking machine either prior to or after being struck by dies. All coins with relief ornamented edges were broadstruck. *See Broadstruck; Edge Marking.*

Oxidation

The result of the combining of oxygen from the air with metal on the surface of a coin or planchet, which occurs either naturally with time or rapidly with heat, as during annealing. *See Patina; Pickling; Scale; Toning.*

Pantograph

A device consisting of hinged levers used to reduce drawings from one size to another by tracing over the larger drawing. It can be very useful in forgery for laying out the patterns for dies, hubs, punches, etc. With practice even a simple pantograph can, in the hands of a skilled operator, successfully engrave incuse patterns for mint marks, date logotypes, lettering, and so forth.

Patina

A thin, hard coating of oxidation or toning that has accumulated on a coin over a long period of time. May range on a bronze coin from a mild, tannish brown to a bright light green. Careful attention to the duplication of patina is very desirable, if not often critical, to a successful forgery.

Pattern

1) The form and composition of the various elements of a coin's design — device, legends, borders, etc. 2) An experimental style for a new coin developed by a mint, but not later issued for circulation. Such patterns are scarce, and some are one of a kind.

Pickling

A mild acid solution used to remove the scale and oxidation that forms on planchets during annealing. Available in dry, granular form from jewelry and lapidary sources. *See Oxidation; Scale.*

Pile

Term applied to the lower of a pair of hammer-striking coin dies. Also called the anvil (as opposed to hammer) die. The pile is generally the obverse die, from its tradition in ancient coinage of being the die with the deepest intaglio relief. Opposite of Trussell.

Pitting

The minute holes and irregular patches on the surface of a coin, caused by oxidation, bronze disease, corrosion, etc. Copper-based coins are particularly vulnerable to pitting, and silver coins somewhat less so, depending upon what has affected them. Gold, of course, does not pit.

Planchet

The blank piece of metal that has been prepared for striking with dies to produce a coin. Earliest planchets were irregular cast lumps; later ancients were cast reasonably round, but still thick. Planchets have been made by hammering metal into thin sheets, by rolling it into sheets, by cutting with snips, chisels, and punches, and have occasionally been filed on to adjust for weight. Planchets for modern coinage are mechanically uniform, earlier types were less so.

Plate Roller

An upright frame supporting a pair of adjustable steel rolling cylinders, which are geared to be turned together by a hand crank on the side of the frame. Used to press strips of annealed metal into thin plates during successive passes. When plate reaches the proper thickness, blanks for planchets can be cut from it. *See Blanking; Ductile.*

Positive

The relief and incuse images of a coin face as they appear on the finished coin, as opposed to the intaglio image of the coin on the coin die.

Prison

A restricted access/egress group care facility where forgers often spend their retirement years, learning to enjoy such recreational activities as showering with members of motorcycle gangs.

Provenance

The "history" of a particular coin, especially if it is rare or in exceptionally fine condition. Does not pertain to the coin's history as a coin per se (where it was made, how much it was valued at, etc.) — but rather to where it was discovered, who has owned it or sold it, what collections it has been in, and so forth. A forger may, of course, attempt to create a fraudulent provenance for a forgery, but this is risky. A more typical way is to create a presumed provenance by careful imitation of fabric.

Punch

A relief engraving on steel of a major device, figure, or element of a coin, which is impressed into a die blank to build up the design of the coin. Predecessor to the hub. Term is also used for tools bearing the image of minor elements, such as individual letters, or the various wedges, curves, and so forth used to compose medieval coin dies. Not to be confused with a blanking punch, which is simply a plain, flat-faced steel rod. *See Device; Hub.*

Quench

A liquid solution of brine, or just cool water, used to "set" the crystalline structure of metal at the point it has reached during heating. For ferrous metals (iron, steel) heated to a high temperature, a quench will harden the metal. For copper based metals, a quench will anneal the metal. *See Annealing; Hardening.*

Reeded Edge

The "gear tooth"-like lands and grooves around the outside edge of some coins, such as the dime and quarter, produced by striking the planchet within a serrated collar. Since the finished coin is ejected straight up from the collar, the vertical reeding is not in the least deformed. The reeded edge is popularly used for a great deal of modern coinage.

Reference Work

A book, like this one, that contains material that is made available to collectors and other interested persons for scholarly and academic purposes only, and which is not intended to encourage anyone to create or do anything illegal.

Relief

Detail in a positive image that is above the surface of the surrounding area. On a Washington quarter, the portrait of Washington is rendered in relief. The opposite of incuse.

Replica (copy)

A private, legitimately produced duplicate of an officially issued coin or other numismatic item, created with the express intent to represent it as a replica to be valued for its intrinsic and artistic merit only. As a demonstration of intent, replicas should be either marked or published as such.

Reverse

The "back" side of a coin, or the side bearing the device regarded by the coin's issuing authority to be of secondary importance to the one on the obverse. With hammer-struck coins, the reverse is normally produced by the upper die, and for machine-struck coinage, the lower die. *See Trussel.*

Rim

The highest part of a modern, machine-struck coin, running around the edge of a coin's faces where the metal of the planchet was forced up along the side of the collar. Dies used in a collar have an intaglio rim cut around them. *See Upset Edge; Wire Rim.*

RTV (room temperature vulcanizing) Silicone Rubber

A 2-part, mixable, pourable rubber compound which cures at room temperature, greatly reducing or eliminating altogether the shrinkage problem normally caused by the heat curing of vulcanized rubber. Ideal for making molds of certain coins for lost wax injection. *See Investment Plaster; Lost Wax Process.*

Scale

1) The thick coating of oxidation on the surface of a piece of metal caused by high heat. Unlike patina, scale is brittle, coarse, and ugly. It is removed by immersion in a pickling solution. 2) The relationship of a representation of an object (as in a drawing, or a model) to the original object, such as 8:1, etc.

Screw Press

1) A statement uttered by Richard Nixon. 2) A machine designed to harness the centrifugal force of a spinning, weighted arm in order to turn a vertical screw and drive coin dies together. Screw presses can produce great force, and due to the relatively slow "pressing" action they employ, dies tend to hold up much better than those subjected to the shock stress of a gravity hammer. A screw press must be quite large though (upwards of 8-10 feet in diameter), to create the force needed for minting even moderate sized coins, and for this reason it is not too practicable for a forger.

Specific Gravity

One of the standard tests performed on coins submitted to authentication services, a coin's weight is compared to the weight of the volume of distilled water equal to that displaced by the coin. By referencing the specific gravity of a coin against the known specific gravity of the alloy the coin is supposed to be made of, it can be determined whether the alloy is, in fact, correct. Many otherwise excellent forgeries have been detected by this simple method because the forger was too lazy to procure or produce a proper planchet.

Sprue

The thin stem of wax connected to a wax model being invested in plaster. The end of the sprue protrudes outside the mold, forming a channel through which the wax is melted out and the molten metal is introduced in.

Stress Hardened (work hardened)

When metal is compressed (as, for instance, by being hammered upon) its molecules are actually forced slightly together, making the metal at the point of impact more dense, and thus harder (less malleable). The less ductile a metal's property is, the more it is capable of being stress hardened. Coins, when struck during the minting process, actually become harder than the planchet from which they were made, as is demonstrated by the effect known as the brockage principle. Many large ancient coins, which had to have been struck multiple times to bring up the high relief detail on them, required annealing between strikes due to stress hardening. *See Annealing; Brockage.*

Strike

The term used when referring to the pressing together of coin dies upon a planchet to produce a coin.

Swedge (swedged, swedging dies)

The shaping of a piece of malleable metal by compressing it within enclosed dies. Technically speaking, all coins struck by upper and lower dies using a restraining collar are swedged, but for the purposes of this book, the term swedging dies refers only to those smooth-faced dies and thick, deep collar well used to produce blank planchets with an artificial upset edge for use in forgery. *See Upset Edge.*

Tempering

The heat treating of metal (generally steel) after it has been hardened so that the object or tool will be less brittle. Tempering will alter the ductility of a metal without increasing its malleability.

Test Cut

Deep, chisel-shaped gouges applied to ancient coins by money changers, merchants, or anyone suspicious of the metallic purity of a coin in the days when plated counterfeits were a nuisance. Such defacing did not alter the intrinsic or commercial value of a coin one whit at the time it was practiced, but modern collectors are appalled by the very thought of it. Needless to say, coins with test cuts are worth less to collectors than those without them — another reason why a forgery with a test cut is less likely to be suspected. *See also Banker's Marks.*

Toning

The discoloration of the metal at the surface of a coin produced by exposure to air, handling, etc. Many older coins, particularly copper ones, are pleasantly toned, even though in an uncirculated condition.

Trial Strike

The impression of a punch, hub, or die upon a piece of metal, made by an engraver at a mint to check the appearance or progress of a design. These are very rare, and yet easily forgeable. A forger cutting his own dies will usually make trial strikes of his own, as well, but of course he will destroy them afterwards.

Trussell

The upper of a pair of hammer-striking coin dies, opposite of pile. Also called the hammer (as opposed to anvil) die. The trussel is usually the reverse die of the coin being struck.

Tumbling

Annealed, pickled, cleaned planchets are often polished by tumbling for several hours in a slowly rotating drum. Any hobby-type rock tumbler can accomplish this for a forger, as well as provide a means to "circulate" finished forgeries for as long as necessary until the desired level of wear is attained.

Type

Term referring to the particular style and design of any particular series of coinage. The Walking Liberty is one type of half dollar; the Lincoln/Memorial cent is one type, the Lincoln/Wheat cent another, etc.

Upset Edge

A thick, raised, rounded rim applied to punched-out planchet blanks prior to striking them into coins within a collar, designed to prolong the life of dies by requiring less pressure to raise the rim for successful strikes. The upset edge is created at mints by compressing the coin's edge between rollers. A forger may do the same, or opt for creating an artificial upset edge using swedging dies. *See Rim; Swedge.*

Wire Rim

A very fine, knifelike burr of metal around the extreme outer edge of a coin that has been struck with excessive pressure within a collar, causing the coin's metal to flow slightly up around the outside edge of the rim shoulder on the die, between the die and the collar. Occasionally found on very soft coins, such as gold, but seldom on harder coins, like nickel alloys. Genuine 1943 bronze cents, struck by accident on presses that had been pre-calibrated to strike steel cents, exhibit a wire rim, whereas many struck forgeries of this coin lack this detail.

X-Ray Spectrography

A sophisticated test performed by authentication services when the exact alloy of a submitted coin must be determined. This is particularly helpful in the case of exotic, unusual, or impure alloys which a forger may not have done enough research on to successfully duplicate.